Scale Smart: Azure A Essentials

First Edition

Preface

The cloud has become the cornerstone of modern computing, fundamentally reshaping how businesses build, deploy, and scale applications. As organizations increasingly migrate from on-premises solutions to the cloud, understanding cloud architecture is not just beneficial—it's essential. This book, **"Scale Smart: Azure Architecture Essentials"**, serves as a foundational manual for anyone looking to grasp the core principles, technologies, and strategies involved in architecting solutions on Microsoft Azure.

The structure of this book has been carefully designed to lead you through a natural progression of understanding, beginning with the basics of cloud architecture and culminating in real-world application and future trends. We start with an exploration of core concepts and architectural fundamentals, then delve into the essential Azure services that serve as building blocks for any scalable and resilient solution. From there, we examine the pillars of modern cloud architecture, including scalability, high availability, security, cost efficiency, and performance monitoring.

Each chapter includes practical insights and architectural guidance specific to Azure, helping bridge the gap between theoretical knowledge and applied best practices. In Chapter 3, for instance, we explore real techniques for scaling applications, while Chapter 4 addresses how to design systems that can withstand failures and recover gracefully. Security and governance, crucial components of any architecture, are explored in depth in Chapter 5.

Cost is always a consideration, which is why Chapter 6 is dedicated entirely to optimization strategies that align architectural choices with business budgets. We then move into modern patterns such as microservices, serverless, and event-driven architectures in Chapter 7. Monitoring and observability, which are vital for long-term success, are covered in Chapter 8.

To ground this knowledge in real-world applications, Chapter 9 includes detailed case studies that walk through how organizations of various sizes and industries use Azure architecture to solve complex problems. Finally, Chapter 10 looks ahead, showcasing innovations like AI integration, edge computing, sustainability, and DevOps—topics that will shape the future of cloud computing.

Whether you're a beginner or an aspiring cloud architect, this book aims to deliver clarity, guidance, and hands-on knowledge that will empower you to build intelligent and effective cloud solutions using Azure.

Let's begin this journey into the world of Azure architecture.

Table of Contents

Chapter 1: Understanding Cloud Architecture Fundamentals

What is Cloud Architecture?

Cloud architecture is the framework that defines the components, systems, and relationships necessary for building, deploying, and managing applications and services in the cloud. It abstracts the underlying infrastructure while offering scalability, flexibility, reliability, and efficiency to support business needs.

In its essence, cloud architecture includes several key elements:

- Front-end and back-end platforms

- Cloud-based delivery

- A network (usually the internet)

- Infrastructure components like storage, compute, and networking

- Services like databases, messaging queues, and monitoring tools

The goal of cloud architecture is not just to move workloads off-premises but to take advantage of cloud-native principles such as automation, elasticity, and distributed design. In a well-architected system, resources are utilized optimally, scaling up or down as needed, and workloads are spread across different geographic regions for redundancy and performance.

Characteristics of Cloud Architecture

- **Elasticity and Scalability:** Resources can scale dynamically with demand.

- **On-Demand Self-Service:** Users can provision resources without human interaction.

- **Resource Pooling:** Multiple tenants share the same resources securely.

- **Broad Network Access:** Services are available over the internet through standard mechanisms.

- **Measured Service:** Cloud systems automatically control and optimize resource use.

These characteristics align with the **five pillars of the Well-Architected Framework**: Cost Optimization, Operational Excellence, Performance Efficiency, Reliability, and Security.

Architectural Models

Cloud computing offers several architectural models. The three most common are:

- **Infrastructure as a Service (IaaS):** Provides virtualized hardware, such as servers and storage. Users manage the OS and applications.

- **Platform as a Service (PaaS):** Provides a platform allowing customers to develop, run, and manage applications without the complexity of building infrastructure.

- **Software as a Service (SaaS):** Delivers software applications over the internet, eliminating the need for installation or maintenance.

Azure supports all three models. For example:

- **IaaS:** Azure Virtual Machines

- **PaaS:** Azure App Services

- **SaaS:** Microsoft 365

Deployment Models

Cloud architecture can also be classified based on deployment models:

- **Public Cloud:** Services are delivered over the public internet and shared across organizations (e.g., Azure).

- **Private Cloud:** Infrastructure is dedicated to a single organization.

- **Hybrid Cloud:** Combines public and private clouds for increased flexibility.

- **Multi-Cloud:** Utilizes services from multiple cloud providers to avoid vendor lock-in.

Each deployment model has implications for design decisions around security, networking, and compliance.

Azure's Approach to Cloud Architecture

Azure's architectural philosophy revolves around three tenets:

1. **Global Infrastructure:** Azure has a large global footprint with multiple data centers in regions across the world. This enables high availability, disaster recovery, and latency optimization.

2. **Security by Design:** Azure integrates security across all layers, from physical data centers to software services, using tools like Azure Security Center, Defender, and role-based access control.

3. **Scalability and Agility:** With services like Azure Kubernetes Service, Azure Functions, and App Service Environments, developers can design architectures that respond quickly to change.

Core Components of Azure Cloud Architecture

Here are some critical components you'll encounter:

- **Compute:** Azure VMs, App Services, Azure Kubernetes Service

- **Storage:** Azure Blob Storage, Files, Tables, Disks

- **Networking:** Virtual Networks (VNets), Network Security Groups, Application Gateways

- **Databases:** Azure SQL Database, Cosmos DB, Azure Database for PostgreSQL

- **Identity:** Azure Active Directory

- **Monitoring:** Azure Monitor, Application Insights

Benefits of Azure Architecture

- **Speed and Agility:** Rapid provisioning and automated deployment pipelines.

- **Resilience and Redundancy:** Built-in availability zones and geo-replication.

- **Security:** Compliance with international standards like ISO, HIPAA, and GDPR.

- **DevOps Integration:** Seamless CI/CD with tools like Azure DevOps and GitHub Actions.

Example: Simple Azure Web Application Architecture

To illustrate a basic Azure architecture, consider a typical three-tier web application:

1. **Frontend (Web App)** – Hosted using Azure App Service.

2. **Backend (API Service)** – Also on Azure App Service or Functions.

3. **Database** – Using Azure SQL Database.

Traffic flows through **Azure Front Door** or **Application Gateway**, which routes requests and provides load balancing and web application firewall capabilities. Monitoring is handled via **Application Insights**, while secrets and configuration settings are stored securely using **Azure Key Vault**.

```
# Example Azure CLI command to create a web app
az webapp create \
  --name mywebapp \
  --resource-group myResourceGroup \
  --plan myAppServicePlan \
  --runtime "DOTNET|6.0"
```

Best Practices for Designing Cloud Architecture

- **Design for failure**: Assume components will fail and architect with redundancy.

- **Use managed services**: Reduce operational complexity and improve scalability.

- **Separate concerns**: Implement microservices or modular design to improve maintainability.

- **Secure everything**: Implement Zero Trust, encrypt data in transit and at rest.

- **Automate everything**: Use Infrastructure as Code (IaC) with Bicep or Terraform.

Conclusion

Understanding cloud architecture sets the stage for every decision you make in Azure. From which service to use, to how you design for failure, to how you monitor and optimize your deployment—every step flows from a strong grasp of architectural principles. Azure's rich set of tools and services allows you to implement these principles effectively, ensuring your solutions are not only functional but also resilient, secure, and scalable. In the chapters that follow, we'll build on these fundamentals and dive deeper into how Azure's core services align with modern architectural best practices.

Key Principles of Scalable Systems

Scalability is a cornerstone of cloud architecture, ensuring that systems can handle increased load without compromising performance or reliability. In the context of Azure and cloud computing in general, scalability means the capability of a system to grow and manage increased demand by provisioning more resources, distributing workloads, and maintaining service quality.

Scalable systems are not accidental—they are intentionally designed with architectural principles that make them elastic, responsive, and resilient. Let's explore these key principles in detail.

Elasticity and On-Demand Provisioning

At the heart of scalability is **elasticity**—the system's ability to automatically adjust resources based on workload demands. This avoids both under-provisioning, which can lead to poor performance or outages, and over-provisioning, which results in unnecessary cost.

Azure supports elasticity through services such as:

- Azure Virtual Machine Scale Sets (VMSS)
- App Service Auto-scaling
- Azure Kubernetes Service (AKS) Horizontal Pod Autoscaler
- Azure Functions with consumption plans

Elastic systems automatically scale out (add resources) when load increases and scale in (remove resources) during low traffic, ensuring cost-efficiency and consistent performance.

```
# Azure CLI command to enable autoscaling for an App Service
az monitor autoscale create \
  --resource-group myResourceGroup \
  --resource myAppServicePlan \
  --resource-type Microsoft.Web/serverfarms \
  --name myAutoscaleSetting \
  --min-count 2 \
  --max-count 10 \
  --count 2
```

Statelessness

Scalable systems must be **stateless**, or at least designed with minimal reliance on internal state. A stateless service processes each request independently, without requiring information from previous interactions. This makes it easier to duplicate instances of the service across servers or containers.

State, if necessary, should be stored in centralized, scalable storage systems such as:

- Azure Blob Storage for files
- Azure Table or Cosmos DB for key-value pairs

- **Azure Redis Cache** for high-speed, in-memory data

Stateless applications are especially beneficial in serverless and container-based architectures where new instances can be rapidly deployed or retired based on load.

Horizontal Scaling

Unlike vertical scaling (adding more resources to a single machine), **horizontal scaling** involves increasing capacity by adding more instances of a component. This form of scaling is more robust, cost-efficient, and aligns with modern cloud-native architectures.

Azure supports horizontal scaling across many services:

- Web Apps in **App Services**
- Containers in **Azure Kubernetes Service**
- Virtual Machines in **Scale Sets**

Horizontal scaling also supports **fault tolerance** because workloads are spread across multiple nodes. If one node fails, the system continues operating with reduced capacity, while new instances are spun up to replace the failed ones.

Load Balancing

A scalable system requires efficient **load distribution** to prevent any single resource from becoming a bottleneck. Load balancers distribute incoming network traffic across multiple backend resources, improving responsiveness and availability.

Azure provides several load balancing options:

- **Azure Load Balancer** (Layer 4)
- **Azure Application Gateway** (Layer 7 with WAF support)
- **Azure Front Door** (Global HTTP/HTTPS load balancing)
- **Traffic Manager** (DNS-based load balancing across regions)

Each load balancer serves different scenarios. For example, use Application Gateway when you need cookie-based session affinity or SSL termination, and Front Door for geo-distribution and global failover.

Loose Coupling

Loosely coupled components are easier to scale independently. In a tightly coupled architecture, a change or failure in one component may affect others. Loose coupling allows each service or module to operate autonomously, interact via APIs or messaging systems, and scale independently.

Azure encourages loose coupling with services such as:

- **Azure**   **Service**   **Bus**
- **Azure**   **Event**   **Grid**
- **Azure**   **Event**   **Hubs**
- **Azure**   **API**   **Management**

These services facilitate asynchronous communication, allowing systems to remain responsive even under heavy load.

Partitioning and Sharding

Large datasets and workloads often need to be **partitioned** (or **sharded**) to scale effectively. Partitioning divides a system's data or responsibilities into segments that can be managed and scaled separately.

Examples in Azure include:

- **Cosmos DB** with partition keys for massive scale-out
- **SQL Database Elastic Pools** for multi-tenant applications
- **Blob Storage Containers** for segregating file sets

Choosing the right partitioning strategy involves understanding access patterns and balancing partitions to avoid hotspots that degrade performance.

Asynchronous Processing

Scalable systems often offload work to background processes using **asynchronous messaging**. This decouples the user experience from long-running tasks and prevents bottlenecks.

Azure provides several mechanisms for asynchronous processing:

- **Azure Queue Storage** for basic message queuing
- **Azure Service Bus Queues and Topics** for enterprise messaging

- **Azure Durable Functions** for orchestrating stateful workflows

These tools support scenarios like order processing, batch file operations, email sending, and data transformation tasks.

Caching

Caching improves system scalability and performance by reducing the load on backend systems. Frequently accessed data is stored in memory, making read operations faster and more scalable.

Azure offers:

- **Azure Cache for Redis** – in-memory data store with sub-millisecond latency

- **Output Caching** in Azure Front Door or CDN

- **Query result caching** in Azure SQL and Cosmos DB

Caching is essential in high-read scenarios such as product catalogs, authentication lookups, or data that changes infrequently.

Idempotency and Retry Logic

As systems scale, the likelihood of **transient failures** increases—timeouts, network glitches, or service throttling. Scalable systems must handle these gracefully using retry policies and **idempotent operations** (where repeating an operation yields the same result).

Azure SDKs and services offer built-in retry mechanisms, and best practice involves:

- Using **Retry-After** headers

- Exponential backoff with jitter

- Circuit breakers to prevent overload

```
// Example: HTTP retry with exponential backoff in JavaScript
async function retryRequest(url, attempts = 5) {
  let delay = 100;
  for (let i = 0; i < attempts; i++) {
    try {
      return await fetch(url);
    } catch (e) {
      if (i === attempts - 1) throw e;
      await new Promise(res => setTimeout(res, delay));
      delay *= 2;
```

```
    }
   }
  }
```

Monitoring and Telemetry

To scale effectively, systems must be observable. **Monitoring**, **logging**, and **telemetry** help detect scaling triggers, failures, and bottlenecks. Azure provides extensive observability tools:

- **Azure** **Monitor** and **Application** **Insights**
- **Log** **Analytics**
- **Azure** **Metrics** **Explorer**
- **Custom** **alerts** **and** **autoscale** **rules**

Effective telemetry enables data-driven decisions, like adjusting scaling rules based on CPU, memory, queue length, or custom business KPIs.

Design for Multi-Tenancy

If you're building a system that serves multiple customers or tenants, scalability must account for **multi-tenancy**. This involves:

- **Data isolation** (per-tenant databases vs shared tables with tenant IDs)
- **Scaling** **policies** **per** **tenant**
- **Rate** **limiting** **or** **throttling** **per** **tenant**

Azure SQL Elastic Pools, Cosmos DB containers with partition keys, and API Management with usage quotas all support multi-tenant scalable architectures.

Cost Awareness and Governance

Scalability must be **cost-aware**. More resources mean more expense, so design decisions should balance performance with efficiency.

Use tools such as:

- **Azure** **Cost** **Management** **+** **Billing**
- **Azure** **Advisor** for cost and performance optimization

- **Budgets   and   alerts**   for   thresholds

- **Tagging   and   resource   groups** for organizing and tracking usage

Rightsizing and autoscaling must align with expected usage patterns, ensuring your architecture grows smartly, not wastefully.

Conclusion

Designing for scalability isn't just about handling more users—it's about ensuring smooth, efficient, and reliable growth. The principles above are the building blocks of robust, cloud-native architecture. Azure offers powerful tools and services that, when used thoughtfully, empower you to scale individual components or entire applications elastically and cost-effectively.

Scalability should be a foundational consideration from the earliest stages of design. When you build systems that are stateless, loosely coupled, observable, and horizontally scalable, you create a resilient architecture ready to meet the demands of tomorrow's users and business challenges. In the next section, we'll dive into how Azure helps you implement these principles through its service offerings.

Overview of Microsoft Azure's Architecture Approach

Microsoft Azure is not just a cloud platform—it's a vast ecosystem of services, principles, and best practices built to support the full lifecycle of cloud-native, hybrid, and enterprise workloads. Azure's architecture is designed to provide global scalability, high availability, strong security, and deep integration capabilities while maintaining flexibility and performance across diverse application types.

Understanding Azure's architectural approach helps developers, architects, and organizations make the most of what the platform offers. In this section, we'll explore the key elements that shape Azure's architectural philosophy, global infrastructure, service organization, availability model, deployment options, and foundational principles for solution design.

Azure's Global Infrastructure

Azure's backbone is its **global infrastructure**, which includes:

- **Geographies**: High-level geopolitical boundaries, often aligned with data residency and   compliance   requirements.

- **Regions**: Physical locations within a geography, each consisting of one or more datacenters. Examples include East US, West Europe, and Southeast Asia.

- **Availability Zones**: Physically separate zones within a region. Each zone has independent power, cooling, and networking, ensuring high availability.

- **Edge Locations**: Points of presence (PoPs) used for content delivery (via CDN) and latency optimization.

This global structure supports architectural patterns like geo-redundancy, low-latency access, and data sovereignty. Services like Azure Front Door and Traffic Manager utilize this structure to deliver performant, region-aware experiences.

```
# Azure CLI command to list available regions
az account list-locations --output table
```

Azure regions are continually expanding, enabling architects to deploy workloads closer to end users, which reduces latency and increases reliability.

Foundational Design Tenets

Azure's architecture adheres to several core principles that guide both platform development and recommended customer architectures:

1. **High**   **Availability**

2. **Scalability**

3. **Security**   **and**   **Compliance**

4. **Performance**   **Optimization**

5. **Cost**   **Efficiency**

6. **Operational**   **Excellence**

These tenets are reflected in the **Microsoft Azure Well-Architected Framework**, which acts as a strategic guide for designing and evaluating systems on Azure.

The Five Pillars of the Azure Well-Architected Framework

Azure's framework is structured around five pillars, each contributing to holistic, resilient cloud solutions:

- **Reliability**: Design for failure, enable auto-recovery, use availability zones and redundancy.

- **Security**: Implement defense in depth, least privilege access, data encryption, and threat detection.

- **Cost Optimization**: Monitor spend, leverage auto-scaling, reserved instances, and cost-effective   services.

- **Operational Excellence**: Use automation, CI/CD, and proper monitoring to ensure smooth   operations.

- **Performance Efficiency**: Use the right resources and scale proactively, not reactively.

These principles are not abstract—they're baked into Azure's services and tools, such as Azure Advisor, which provides personalized recommendations for improvement across these dimensions.

Service Model: Azure's Platform Architecture

Azure organizes its vast set of services into several key categories that align with modern architectural patterns:

- **Compute**: Azure Virtual Machines, Azure App Services, Azure Kubernetes Service (AKS),   Azure   Functions

- **Storage**: Azure Blob Storage, File Storage, Disk Storage, Archive Storage

- **Databases**: Azure SQL Database, Cosmos DB, Azure Database for PostgreSQL/MySQL/MariaDB

- **Networking**: VNets, VPN Gateway, ExpressRoute, Azure DNS, Load Balancer, Application   Gateway

- **Identity**:   Azure   Active   Directory,   Azure   AD   B2C

- **AI + Machine Learning**: Azure Cognitive Services, Azure Machine Learning

- **DevOps**:   Azure   DevOps   Services,   GitHub   Actions,   Azure   Pipelines

- **Monitoring & Management**: Azure Monitor, Application Insights, Azure Log Analytics

- **Security**: Microsoft Defender for Cloud, Key Vault, Azure Firewall, Azure Policy

These services are modular and composable. Architects can build simple to highly complex solutions by combining multiple services to meet the specific needs of their applications.

High Availability and Fault Isolation

Azure offers **built-in availability options** to ensure systems remain functional even in the face of localized failures. These include:

- **Availability Sets**: Logical groupings of VMs to protect against hardware failures within a datacenter.

- **Availability Zones**: Provide higher redundancy across physical zones. Applications can distribute workloads across zones for mission-critical availability.

- **Geo-Redundancy**: Services like Azure Storage and SQL Database offer geo-replication for DR scenarios.

```
# Create a VM in an Availability Set
az vm availability-set create \
  --name myAvailabilitySet \
  --resource-group myResourceGroup \
  --platform-fault-domain-count 2 \
  --platform-update-domain-count 2
```

By designing for fault isolation and recovery, Azure enables highly available applications even under unpredictable conditions.

Deployment and Resource Management

Azure uses **Resource Groups** to manage and logically group related services. These groups act as units of deployment, access control, and lifecycle management.

Infrastructure can be provisioned using:

- **Azure Portal** (UI-based)

- **Azure CLI** (scripting)

- **PowerShell**

- **ARM Templates** (declarative JSON)

- **Bicep** (more readable syntax for ARM)

- **Terraform** (third-party IaC tool)

```
# Deploy resources using Bicep
az deployment group create \
  --resource-group myResourceGroup \
  --template-file main.bicep
```

Resource organization is critical for governance, especially in large-scale environments with many teams and services.

Azure Resource Manager (ARM)

At the heart of Azure's architecture is the **Azure Resource Manager (ARM)**. ARM provides:

- A unified management layer
- Role-based access control (RBAC)
- Tags and policies
- Dependency management
- Support for templates and IaC

All interactions with Azure services—whether via CLI, Portal, or SDK—go through ARM, ensuring consistent behavior, auditability, and governance.

Azure's Shared Responsibility Model

Azure follows a **shared responsibility model**, which clearly delineates the responsibilities of Microsoft and the customer:

- **Microsoft's Responsibility**: Physical infrastructure, network, hypervisor, host OS, and some managed services.
- **Customer's Responsibility**: Data, applications, identity, endpoints, configurations.

Depending on the service model (IaaS, PaaS, SaaS), the responsibility balance shifts. For example, IaaS customers must manage their own OS patches and firewalls, whereas in PaaS, Azure handles much of that automatically.

Integration and Extensibility

Azure is designed to be **open and extensible**, supporting integration with:

- **Third-party tools and platforms** (e.g., Splunk, Datadog, Terraform)
- **Hybrid environments** (Azure Arc, VPN Gateway, ExpressRoute)
- **DevOps pipelines** (GitHub, Jenkins, Azure DevOps)
- **Programming languages** (Python, JavaScript, .NET, Go, Java)

This flexibility allows teams to use their preferred tools while leveraging Azure's infrastructure and services.

Multi-Cloud and Hybrid Architecture

Azure supports hybrid and multi-cloud strategies via:

- **Azure Arc**: Manage and govern resources across clouds and on-premises.

- **Azure Stack**: Run Azure services on-premises.

- **Azure Lighthouse**: Cross-tenant management for service providers.

- **Azure VMware Solution**: Extend VMware environments into Azure.

These tools help organizations avoid vendor lock-in, comply with data residency regulations, and modernize at their own pace.

Governance, Compliance, and Policy

Large enterprises need to maintain control over sprawling cloud resources. Azure offers governance tools such as:

- **Azure Policy**: Enforce organizational rules (e.g., prevent deployment of public IPs).

- **Azure Blueprints**: Predefined configurations including RBAC, policies, and ARM templates.

- **Management Groups**: Organize subscriptions for unified policy application.

- **Tags**: Organize resources for cost tracking, security boundaries, and project management.

Azure complies with dozens of international, regional, and industry-specific standards including **HIPAA, ISO 27001, FedRAMP, GDPR**, and more.

Monitoring and Operational Insight

Azure provides powerful built-in monitoring tools:

- **Azure Monitor**: Centralized metrics, logs, and alerts

- **Application Insights**: APM for custom applications

- **Log Analytics**: Advanced query capabilities over collected data

- **Azure Advisor**: Recommendations to improve availability, security, and performance

These tools enable proactive operations, helping you identify bottlenecks, misconfigurations, or cost spikes before they become problems.

Conclusion

Microsoft Azure's architectural approach is vast, yet deeply integrated. It's built to scale with your ambitions—whether you're launching a simple website, deploying a global SaaS platform, or modernizing a legacy enterprise stack.

By leveraging Azure's global infrastructure, service diversity, automation tools, and best-practice frameworks, you can create architectures that are resilient, secure, performant, and cost-effective. Understanding this approach is the first step in transforming ideas into scalable, production-ready solutions in the cloud.

In the following chapters, we'll break down these components and show you how to architect and implement systems that not only meet your needs today but also adapt and grow alongside your organization's goals.

Chapter 2: Core Azure Services and Their Architectural Roles

Compute Services: VMs, App Services, and Containers

Compute is the backbone of most applications. Whether you're running a monolithic enterprise application, a set of microservices, or serverless APIs, Azure offers a variety of compute services to match different architectural needs. The choice between these services—**Virtual Machines**, **App Services**, and **Containers**—has profound implications on performance, scalability, cost, and maintainability.

This section explores how each compute service works, their architectural fit, use cases, and integration patterns within broader Azure solutions.

Azure Virtual Machines (VMs)

Azure VMs offer Infrastructure as a Service (IaaS), allowing full control over the OS, software, and configurations. This model is ideal for:

- Migrating   legacy   applications

- Running   custom   workloads   not   supported   by   PaaS

- Situations   where   deep   system-level   control   is   required

VMs can be provisioned in various sizes (Standard_B, Dv5, Ev4, etc.), with support for both Linux and Windows operating systems. They can be integrated into **Availability Sets** or **Availability Zones** for high availability, and with **VM Scale Sets** for horizontal scaling.

```
# Create a basic VM using Azure CLI
az vm create \
  --resource-group MyResourceGroup \
  --name MyVM \
  --image UbuntuLTS \
  --admin-username azureuser \
  --generate-ssh-keys
```

Architectural Implications:

- Requires   patching,   updates,   and   OS   maintenance

- Full   responsibility   for   scaling   and   load   balancing

- Suitable for tightly coupled systems or custom stack requirements

Azure App Services

App Services provide a Platform as a Service (PaaS) environment for hosting web applications, RESTful APIs, and mobile backends. You can deploy apps using .NET, Node.js, Java, Python, PHP, and Ruby with seamless CI/CD from GitHub or Azure Repos.

Key capabilities include:

- **Built-in load balancing**
- **Custom domains and SSL certificates**
- **Auto-scaling and deployment slots**
- **App Service Environment (ASE)** for isolated and high-performance needs

```
# Deploy a web app using App Service
az webapp up --name MyUniqueAppName --resource-group MyResourceGroup --runtime "NODE|18-lts"
```

Architectural Implications:

- Abstracts infrastructure concerns
- Built-in high availability and scaling
- Ideal for stateless, scalable web applications
- Limited access to underlying OS or system-level configurations

App Services support both **Linux** and **Windows** plans and integrate with services like **Azure Monitor**, **Key Vault**, **App Configuration**, and **Application Insights** for a complete observability and governance experience.

Containers with Azure Kubernetes Service (AKS) and Azure Container Instances (ACI)

Containers represent a lightweight, portable, and efficient compute option. Azure offers multiple services for managing containerized workloads:

Azure Kubernetes Service (AKS)

AKS is a managed Kubernetes service that simplifies deploying, managing, and scaling containerized applications using Kubernetes. It abstracts the complexity of managing a Kubernetes control plane, letting you focus on your applications.

Use cases include:

- Microservices   architecture

- Hybrid   workloads

- Workloads   requiring   orchestration,   autoscaling,   and   service   discovery

Key features:

- Native   integration   with   Azure   Monitor,   Key   Vault,   and   AD

- Network   policy   support   for   security   and   compliance

- CI/CD   with   GitHub   Actions   and   Azure   DevOps

- Horizontal   Pod   Autoscaler   and   Cluster   Autoscaler

```
# Create an AKS cluster
az aks create \
  --resource-group MyResourceGroup \
  --name MyAKSCluster \
  --node-count 3 \
  --enable-addons monitoring \
  --generate-ssh-keys
```

Architectural Implications:

- Suited   for   highly   scalable   and   distributed   systems

- Requires   understanding   of   Kubernetes   architecture

- More flexible but with increased operational overhead compared to App Services

Azure Container Instances (ACI)

ACI allows you to run containers without orchestrators or infrastructure management. This is a serverless container solution ideal for:

- Event-driven   background   tasks

- Data   processing   jobs

- Quick   test   environments

```
# Deploy a container to ACI
az container create \
  --resource-group MyResourceGroup \
  --name MyContainer \
  --image mcr.microsoft.com/azuredocs/aci-helloworld \
  --dns-name-label mycontainerdns \
  --ports 80
```

Architectural Implications:

- Extremely   fast   startup   and   pay-per-second   billing

- No   orchestration—limited   to   single   container   group

- Integrates   well   with   Event   Grid,   Logic   Apps,   and   Functions

Comparing Compute Options

Feature	Azure VMs	Azure App Services	AKS (Kubernetes)	ACI
Control Level	High	Medium	High	Low
Scalability	Manual / Scale Sets	Auto-scaling built-in	Auto-scaling with HPA/CA	Quick-start, manual scaling
Best for	Legacy apps, custom OS	Web apps, APIs	Microservices, containers	One-off jobs, lightweight apps
OS Management	Manual	Handled by Azure	Partial (worker nodes only)	N/A
Orchestration	Manual or Azure services	N/A	Kubernetes	None
Startup Time	Minutes	Seconds	Minutes	Seconds

Selecting the Right Compute Service

Choosing the right compute option requires evaluating trade-offs between control, scalability, cost, and maintenance. Consider the following:

- **Use Azure VMs** when you need full system access, legacy compatibility, or custom stack installations.

- **Use App Services** for rapid deployment of stateless web applications, especially if you're building REST APIs or customer-facing sites.

- **Use AKS** for complex microservice applications, especially when orchestration, DevOps, and CI/CD pipelines are core requirements.

- **Use ACI** for short-lived, event-driven, or ad hoc container execution needs.

Compute in Hybrid Architectures

Azure supports hybrid compute scenarios via:

- **Azure Arc**: Enables Kubernetes and VM management across on-premises, multi-cloud, and edge.

- **Azure Stack Hub/Edge**: Extends Azure capabilities to disconnected environments.

- **ExpressRoute**: Provides private connectivity between Azure and on-premises networks.

These capabilities help organizations modernize applications incrementally while maintaining control over compliance and latency-sensitive workloads.

Observability and Management Tools

All compute services integrate with Azure's monitoring and management suite:

- **Azure Monitor** for metrics and logs

- **Application Insights** for distributed tracing

- **Log Analytics** for querying telemetry data

- **Azure Advisor** for cost, performance, and security recommendations

Compute management is further enhanced through:

- **Auto-scaling rules**

- Runbooks   via   **Azure**   **Automation**

- Role-based   access   controls   (RBAC)

- Policy   enforcement   via   **Azure**   **Policy**

DevOps Integration

All compute services are CI/CD ready. You can:

- Deploy App Services directly from GitHub or Azure DevOps.

- Use **Helm** or **Kustomize** for AKS deployments.

- Trigger ACI jobs from Logic Apps or Event Grid.

Azure's developer ecosystem ensures your compute strategy aligns with modern DevOps pipelines, infrastructure as code, and GitOps principles.

Conclusion

Azure's compute services provide a spectrum of choices, from full control to complete abstraction. Whether you're lifting-and-shifting legacy workloads into VMs, deploying modern APIs using App Services, or orchestrating containers with AKS, Azure offers scalable, secure, and integrated solutions.

Understanding the capabilities, use cases, and trade-offs of each compute option is essential for crafting effective, maintainable cloud architectures. In the next sections, we'll explore how storage, networking, and databases complement these compute services to form the foundation of complete, resilient cloud-native systems on Azure.

Storage Solutions: Blob, Table, Queue, and File Storage

In any cloud architecture, storage plays a central role. Whether you're hosting application data, media files, logs, user-generated content, telemetry, or backups, the ability to store and retrieve data efficiently, securely, and scalably is essential. Microsoft Azure offers a robust set of storage services designed to meet the needs of modern applications across a wide array of use cases. In this section, we'll dive into four of the most critical storage solutions in Azure: **Blob Storage**, **Table Storage**, **Queue Storage**, and **File Storage**.

Each of these storage types supports specific workloads and architectural patterns, from unstructured binary data to structured NoSQL tables and reliable messaging queues. Understanding when and how to use each can lead to more efficient, performant, and cost-effective cloud applications.

Azure Blob Storage

Azure Blob Storage is Microsoft's object storage solution for the cloud. It is ideal for storing large amounts of unstructured data—such as text or binary data—including documents, images, video, backups, and logs.

Key Features:

- **Three access tiers**: Hot, Cool, and Archive, optimizing for usage patterns and cost.

- **Supports REST APIs and SDKs** for most major languages.

- **Scalable to petabytes of data**, with high availability.

- **Supports Azure Data Lake Storage Gen2** for big data analytics.

- **Immutable storage policies** for compliance and security.

Blob Storage organizes data into containers, which are similar to folders. Within containers, you can store blobs in one of three types:

- **Block Blobs**: Ideal for files, media, and documents.

- **Append Blobs**: Optimized for append-only operations such as logs.

- **Page Blobs**: Used primarily for Azure VMs and their virtual hard disks (VHDs).

```
# Create a storage account and a container using Azure CLI
az storage account create --name mystorageacct --resource-group myResourceGroup --location eastus --sku Standard_LRS

az storage container create --name mycontainer --account-name mystorageacct --public-access off
```

Blob Storage is well-suited for use in content delivery networks (CDNs), static website hosting, big data pipelines, and backups.

Azure Table Storage

Table Storage provides a NoSQL key-value store that is highly scalable and cost-effective. It's optimized for fast, flexible access to large quantities of structured, non-relational data. Each record in Table Storage is a set of properties (columns) stored as an entity with a unique **PartitionKey** and **RowKey**.

Use Cases:

- Storing user profiles, device metadata, session logs.

- Lightweight data storage for IoT systems.

- Auditing and diagnostic logs.

- Multi-tenant SaaS applications with partitioned data.

Benefits:

- Schema-less design allows rapid iteration.

- Efficient for lookups by primary key.

- Integrates seamlessly with other Azure services.

```
# Insert data into a table using Azure CLI and PowerShell
az storage entity insert \
  --entity PartitionKey=users RowKey=001 Name="Alice" Email="alice@example.com" \
  --account-name mystorageacct --table-name UserProfiles
```

Because of its simple design and high throughput, Table Storage is a good fit when relationships between data are minimal and the application logic handles much of the processing.

Azure Queue Storage

Queue Storage offers cloud-based message queuing that enables asynchronous message exchange between application components. It's designed for high-throughput, reliable messaging with low latency.

Each message in the queue can be up to 64 KB in size (or up to 7 MB using large message support with base64 encoding), and queues can contain millions of messages.

Architectural Scenarios:

- Decoupling microservices or application tiers.

- Implementing background job processing.

- Buffering high-volume incoming requests.

- Queue-based load leveling and retry logic.

Key Capabilities:

- Simple FIFO queue semantics.

- Visibility timeouts and message TTL.

- Poison message handling (dead-lettering).

```
# Add a message to a queue
az storage message put \
  --account-name mystorageacct \
  --queue-name myqueue \
  --content "ProcessOrder:12345"
```

Queues allow backend workers to process tasks asynchronously, reducing the load on front-end systems and improving responsiveness.

Azure File Storage

Azure Files provides fully managed file shares in the cloud, accessible via the standard SMB (Server Message Block) protocol. This enables file sharing across VMs and services using a familiar interface, which is especially useful for lift-and-shift scenarios and legacy applications.

Features:

- SMB and NFS support for Windows and Linux clients.

- Can be mounted concurrently by cloud or on-prem systems.

- Supports Azure AD-based authentication.

- Offers Premium tier with high IOPS and low latency.

Use Cases:

- Shared file systems for apps and microservices.

- Centralized logs and configuration files.

- Lift-and-shift applications needing legacy support.

- Persistent file storage for containers.

```
# Mounting Azure File Share on Linux
sudo mount -t cifs //mystorageacct.file.core.windows.net/myshare /mnt/myshare \
```

-o
vers=3.0,username=mystorageacct,password=STORAGE_KEY,dir_mode=0777,file_mode=0777,serverino

Azure File Sync can also be used to synchronize on-prem file servers with Azure Files, supporting hybrid cloud architectures and DR strategies.

Storage Redundancy Options

All Azure Storage services support various redundancy models to ensure durability and high availability:

- **Locally Redundant Storage (LRS)**: Replicates data within a single region.

- **Zone-Redundant Storage (ZRS)**: Replicates across multiple availability zones.

- **Geo-Redundant Storage (GRS)**: Replicates to a secondary region, hundreds of miles away.

- **Read-Access Geo-Redundant Storage (RA-GRS)**: Same as GRS, but with read access to the secondary location.

Redundancy options directly impact cost and recovery capabilities, making it important to choose based on business continuity requirements.

Integration and Security

Azure Storage integrates natively with:

- **Azure Active Directory** and **role-based access control (RBAC)**
- **Azure Key Vault** for key and secret management
- **Private Endpoints** for network isolation
- **Azure Policy** for compliance enforcement
- **Azure Monitor** and **Log Analytics** for metrics and diagnostics

Data can be encrypted at rest using Microsoft-managed keys or customer-managed keys (CMK), and in transit using HTTPS.

Cost Management and Performance

To optimize cost:

- Use **Hot** tier for frequently accessed data.

- Use **Cool** tier for infrequently accessed data (minimum storage duration applies).

- Use **Archive** tier for rarely accessed, long-term storage (high retrieval latency).

You can also monitor usage and apply lifecycle policies to automatically transition data between tiers.

```
{
  "rules": [
    {
      "enabled": true,
      "name": "archive-old-blobs",
      "type": "Lifecycle",
      "definition": {
        "filters": {
          "blobTypes": ["blockBlob"],
          "prefixMatch": ["logs/"]
        },
        "actions": {
          "baseBlob": {
            "tierToArchive": {
              "daysAfterModificationGreaterThan": 30
            }
          }
        }
      }
    }
  ]
}
```

This sample lifecycle rule automatically archives blobs older than 30 days under the logs/ path.

Choosing the Right Storage Solution

Use Case	Recommended Service
Static website hosting	Azure Blob Storage
Asynchronous messaging	Azure Queue Storage
Key-value storage for user data	Azure Table Storage

File sharing between applications	Azure File Storage
Long-term archival data	Blob Storage (Archive)
High-throughput analytics	Blob Storage + Data Lake
Legacy application migration	Azure Files

Choosing the right storage type involves analyzing access patterns, performance needs, and cost constraints. For most cloud-native apps, a combination of services will be used across the stack.

Conclusion

Azure's storage solutions provide a comprehensive toolkit for every architectural requirement, whether you're building real-time applications, processing large data sets, enabling legacy integration, or designing for the future. By understanding how each storage type functions and integrates within the Azure ecosystem, architects can make informed decisions that enhance performance, ensure resilience, and reduce costs.

As we move forward, you'll see how these storage services play vital roles in Azure's networking, database, and compute offerings. Together, they form the backbone of scalable, secure, and reliable cloud architectures.

Networking Essentials: VNets, Load Balancers, and Traffic Manager

Effective networking is the glue that binds together all components of a cloud architecture. In Microsoft Azure, networking isn't just about connectivity—it's about control, security, performance, and scalability. Azure's networking services are powerful and flexible, supporting everything from basic web apps to globally distributed, enterprise-grade systems.

In this section, we explore the foundational components of Azure networking: **Virtual Networks (VNets)**, **Load Balancers**, and **Traffic Manager**. These are essential for architecting secure, performant, and resilient solutions in the cloud.

Azure Virtual Network (VNet)

A **Virtual Network (VNet)** in Azure is the fundamental building block of private network space in the cloud. It allows Azure resources like virtual machines, containers, databases, and application services to securely communicate with each other, the internet, and on-premises networks.

Key Characteristics:

- VNets are **region-specific**.

- Each VNet can be segmented using **subnets**.

- VNets provide **IP address ranges** (private IPv4 or IPv6).

- Supports custom DNS, routing tables, and **network security groups (NSGs)**.

```
# Create a VNet with two subnets
az network vnet create \
 --name myVNet \
 --resource-group myResourceGroup \
 --address-prefix 10.0.0.0/16 \
 --subnet-name frontendSubnet \
 --subnet-prefix 10.0.1.0/24

az network vnet subnet create \
 --vnet-name myVNet \
 --name backendSubnet \
 --resource-group myResourceGroup \
 --address-prefix 10.0.2.0/24
```

VNets enable **isolated** and **controlled** communication. You can enforce network rules through:

- **NSGs**: Filter inbound and outbound traffic at the subnet or NIC level.

- **Route Tables**: Override default Azure routing behavior.

- **Service Endpoints**: Provide direct connection to Azure services over the backbone network.

- **Private Endpoints**: Enable private access to Azure PaaS services (e.g., Azure Storage, SQL Database) without exposing them to the public internet.

Hybrid Connectivity:

- **VPN Gateway**: Site-to-site VPN connections to on-premises.

- **Azure ExpressRoute**: Dedicated private fiber connection for high throughput and low latency.

- **VNet Peering**: Seamless and private network communication between VNets in the same or different regions.

With **VNet Peering**, resources communicate across VNets as if they were on the same network.

```
# Peer two VNets
az network vnet peering create \
  --name myVNet1-to-myVNet2 \
  --resource-group myResourceGroup \
  --vnet-name myVNet1 \
  --remote-vnet                                    /subscriptions/<sub-
id>/resourceGroups/myResourceGroup/providers/Microsoft.Network/virtualNetworks/myVNe
t2 \
  --allow-vnet-access
```

Azure Load Balancer

Azure Load Balancer provides Layer 4 (TCP, UDP) distribution of incoming traffic across multiple backend resources. It's commonly used to distribute traffic to virtual machines, virtual machine scale sets, or other compute resources.

Types:

- **Public Load Balancer**: Routes internet traffic to VMs or services.

- **Internal Load Balancer (ILB)**: Routes traffic within a VNet, useful for internal line-of-business applications.

Key Features:

- Supports **TCP/UDP health probes** for instance health detection.

- Enables **high availability** and **fault tolerance**.

- Integrates with **VM scale sets** for dynamic scaling.

- Offers **zonal redundancy** and **HA ports** for high-throughput scenarios.

```
# Create a basic public load balancer
az network lb create \
  --resource-group myResourceGroup \
  --name myLoadBalancer \
  --sku Standard \
  --frontend-ip-name myFrontEnd \
  --backend-pool-name myBackEndPool \
  --public-ip-address myPublicIP
```

Load Balancer is stateless and does not maintain session affinity. For more advanced HTTP/S routing or SSL offloading, use Application Gateway or Front Door.

Application Gateway vs. Load Balancer

While Load Balancer handles raw TCP/UDP traffic, **Azure Application Gateway** operates at Layer 7 (HTTP/HTTPS). It provides:

- **Path-based** routing
- **URL** rewrites and redirection
- **SSL** termination and end-to-end TLS
- **Web** Application Firewall (WAF)

It's ideal for web applications needing advanced routing, traffic inspection, and security features.

Azure Traffic Manager

Traffic Manager is a DNS-based traffic load balancer. It does not route traffic directly but returns the appropriate endpoint based on a configured routing method.

Use Cases:

- Distribute traffic across multiple regions.
- Enable active-active or active-passive failover.
- Improve performance by geo-location or lowest latency.

Routing Methods:

- **Priority**: Route traffic to a primary endpoint, failover to secondary.
- **Weighted**: Route traffic proportionally based on assigned weights.
- **Performance**: Direct users to the closest endpoint in terms of latency.
- **Geographic**: Route based on user geographic location.
- **Multivalue**: Return multiple healthy endpoints.
- **Subnet**: Map user IP ranges to specific endpoints.

```
# Create a Traffic Manager profile
az network traffic-manager profile create \
  --name myTrafficManagerProfile \
  --resource-group myResourceGroup \
  --routing-method Performance \
  --unique-dns-name mytrafficmanager \
  --ttl 30 \
  --monitor-path "/" \
  --monitor-port 80 \
  --monitor-protocol HTTP
```

Traffic Manager enables **global redundancy**, **resilience**, and **geographic optimization**, often used in combination with Azure Front Door or CDN.

Network Security and Governance

Azure networking services are deeply integrated with governance and security tools:

- **Network Security Groups (NSGs)**: Enforce granular traffic filtering.

- **Azure Firewall**: Stateful, fully managed firewall with logging and policy enforcement.

- **Private Link**: Access Azure services privately via your VNet.

- **DDoS Protection**: Automatic and enhanced protection against distributed denial-of-service attacks.

- **Azure Policy**: Enforce network configuration standards.

Using NSGs, for example, you can control access to subnets and VMs:

```
# Create an NSG rule to allow port 80
az network nsg rule create \
  --resource-group myResourceGroup \
  --nsg-name myNSG \
  --name AllowHTTP \
  --priority 100 \
  --destination-port-ranges 80 \
  --protocol Tcp \
  --access Allow \
  --direction Inbound
```

Observability and Diagnostics

Proper observability of network traffic is crucial in any architecture. Azure provides:

- **Network Watcher**: Analyze traffic flow, monitor NSG rules, and troubleshoot VPNs.

- **Connection Monitor**: Track the availability and latency of connections.

- **NSG Flow Logs**: Monitor and archive VNet traffic flows to Azure Storage.

- **Azure Monitor and Log Analytics**: Centralized metric and log analysis.

With these tools, you can understand the flow of traffic, troubleshoot bottlenecks, and validate compliance with security policies.

Design Considerations

When designing Azure networking architecture:

- **Isolate environments** using separate VNets or subnets (e.g., dev/test/prod).

- Use **VNet Peering** instead of VPN where low-latency is required.

- Segment tiers (web, app, database) with **subnets and NSGs**.

- Ensure **high availability** with **Load Balancer** or **Application Gateway**.

- Use **Traffic Manager** for multi-region or geo-failover designs.

- Leverage **Private Endpoints** for secure access to PaaS services.

- Automate networking deployments using ARM, Bicep, or Terraform.

Conclusion

Networking in Azure is a vast and powerful domain. By mastering VNets, Load Balancers, and Traffic Manager, architects can design systems that are secure, resilient, and globally accessible. These services, combined with Azure's governance, observability, and hybrid connectivity capabilities, offer unmatched flexibility to support nearly any application architecture.

As your solutions scale, your network must scale too—intelligently, securely, and efficiently. These foundational services make it possible to architect modern cloud-native applications that meet the highest standards of reliability, performance, and compliance.

Database Options: SQL Database, Cosmos DB, and Azure Database for PostgreSQL

Data is at the heart of nearly every application. Whether you're managing structured, semi-structured, or unstructured data, selecting the right database service is critical for scalability, availability, performance, and security. Azure offers a broad range of database solutions, each tailored to specific workloads and architectural goals. In this section, we explore three of the most prominent options: **Azure SQL Database**, **Azure Cosmos DB**, and **Azure Database for PostgreSQL**.

Each service supports modern app development and integrates seamlessly into Azure's ecosystem. Understanding their capabilities and limitations is essential for making informed architecture decisions.

Azure SQL Database

Azure SQL Database is a fully managed Platform as a Service (PaaS) relational database engine based on Microsoft SQL Server. It supports most of the SQL Server features developers are familiar with, such as T-SQL, stored procedures, and triggers, but with the advantages of automatic patching, backups, and scaling.

Key Features:

- **Automatic tuning and performance optimization**

- **Built-in high availability and geo-replication**

- **Elastic pools for multi-tenant SaaS applications**

- **Advanced security features** including Always Encrypted, TDE, and auditing

- **Integration with Azure Active Directory and Key Vault**

Azure SQL is available in two main deployment options:

- **Single Database**: Ideal for isolated workloads.

- **Elastic Pool**: Designed to share resources across multiple databases.

Provisioning Example:

```
# Create an Azure SQL server and a database
az sql server create \
  --name mySqlServer \
  --resource-group myResourceGroup \
  --location eastus \
  --admin-user myadmin \
  --admin-password MyP@ssw0rd123

az sql db create \
  --resource-group myResourceGroup \
```

```
--server mySqlServer \
--name myDatabase \
--service-objective S1
```

Use Cases:

- OLTP systems

- Line-of-business applications

- ERP and CRM platforms

- Web and API backends with relational data

SQL Database also supports **Hyperscale** for workloads that require fast scaling beyond the traditional size limits of SQL engines, making it suitable for large-scale enterprise systems.

Azure Cosmos DB

Azure Cosmos DB is a globally distributed, multi-model NoSQL database service designed for high availability, ultra-low latency, and horizontal scaling. It supports multiple APIs and data models, including:

- **Core (SQL) API**

- **MongoDB API**

- **Gremlin (graph) API**

- **Cassandra API**

- **Table API**

Standout Features:

- **Guaranteed low latency** (single-digit millisecond reads and writes)

- **99.999% availability SLAs**

- **Multi-region writes and reads**

- **Five consistency models**, from strong to eventual

- **Automatic indexing and schema-free design**

Cosmos DB is ideal for applications that demand high throughput and low latency globally.

Creating a Cosmos DB Account:

```
# Create a Cosmos DB account with SQL API
az cosmosdb create \
  --name myCosmosAccount \
  --resource-group myResourceGroup \
  --kind GlobalDocumentDB \
  --locations regionName=eastus failoverPriority=0 \
  --default-consistency-level Session
```

Use Cases:

- IoT and telemetry data

- Personalized recommendation engines

- Ecommerce and real-time inventory systems

- Global applications requiring low-latency access

- Event sourcing and streaming pipelines

Cosmos DB is schema-agnostic, allowing for rapid development and adaptation, especially for applications with frequently evolving data structures.

Azure Database for PostgreSQL

Azure Database for PostgreSQL is a managed relational database service based on the open-source PostgreSQL engine. It supports two major deployment models:

- **Single Server** (classic, with built-in high availability)

- **Flexible Server** (recommended for most scenarios due to greater control and scalability)

Key Capabilities:

- Support for popular PostgreSQL extensions (e.g., PostGIS)

- Fine-grained VNet and private endpoint integration

- Automatic backups with point-in-time restore

- Zone-redundant high availability (Flexible Server)

- Read   replicas   for   horizontal   read   scaling

Provisioning a Flexible Server:

```
# Create a PostgreSQL flexible server
az postgres flexible-server create \
  --resource-group myResourceGroup \
  --name mypgserver \
  --location eastus \
  --admin-user pgadmin \
  --admin-password MyP@ssw0rd123 \
  --sku-name Standard_B1ms
```

Use Cases:

- Geospatial applications using PostGIS

- Analytics platforms and reporting systems

- Open-source application backends (e.g., Django, Ruby on Rails)

- Financial and transactional systems requiring ACID compliance

The flexible server model also allows developers to control maintenance windows, configure custom time zones, and scale compute and storage independently.

Comparative Overview

Feature	SQL Database	Cosmos DB	PostgreSQL (Flexible)
Type	Relational	NoSQL, Multi-Model	Relational
Scale	Vertical + Hyperscale	Horizontal (global)	Vertical (scalable nodes)
Best For	Traditional apps, OLTP	IoT, real-time apps, NoSQL	Open-source web apps, GIS
Multi-Region Support	Read-only replicas	Read and write	Read replicas (in preview)
ACID Transactions	Yes	Yes (limited scope)	Yes

Schema	Rigid (schema-first)	Schema-less	Flexible (schema-first)
API Access	T-SQL	SQL, MongoDB, Cassandra	SQL (PostgreSQL)
Pricing Model	DTU/vCore-based	RU/s-based	vCore-based

Choosing the Right Database Service

The right database depends on your specific application needs:

- **Choose Azure SQL Database** if you need mature relational database capabilities, transactional consistency, and enterprise security features.

- **Choose Cosmos DB** for apps needing distributed architecture, high availability, and flexible schemas.

- **Choose Azure Database for PostgreSQL** if you prefer open-source ecosystems and require complex querying with extensibility (e.g., spatial analysis).

Many real-world applications use multiple databases. For example, a global SaaS platform might use:

- Azure SQL Database for billing and customer data
- Cosmos DB for real-time activity streams
- PostgreSQL for backend analytics and reporting

This **polyglot persistence** approach allows each component to use the optimal database model.

Security, Compliance, and Integration

All three databases support:

- **Encryption at rest and in transit**
- **Integration with Azure Active Directory**
- **Private endpoints and VNet integration**
- **Role-based access control (RBAC)**

- **Geo-redundant** **backups**

They are compliant with major industry standards including **ISO 27001**, **SOC 1/2/3**, **GDPR**, **HIPAA**, and **FedRAMP**, making them suitable for highly regulated environments.

Integration is also a strength across all three:

- Connect to **Azure Logic Apps**, **Azure Functions**, and **Power BI**
- Stream data into **Azure Data Lake** or **Synapse Analytics**
- Secure secrets and credentials with **Azure Key Vault**

Backup, Restore, and High Availability

Each service offers built-in high availability and backup strategies:

- **SQL Database** supports automatic backups and geo-restore.
- **Cosmos DB** provides multi-region writes and point-in-time restore.
- **PostgreSQL Flexible Server** offers automated backups and zone-redundant HA.

These features are crucial for disaster recovery and business continuity planning.

Conclusion

Azure's database portfolio empowers architects and developers to build applications that are performant, secure, and scalable—regardless of data shape or structure. Whether you need the power of relational databases, the flexibility of NoSQL, or the control of open-source engines, Azure has a solution to fit your needs.

By understanding the strengths and trade-offs of Azure SQL Database, Cosmos DB, and PostgreSQL, you can design data layers that align with your application's scale, availability, and workload characteristics. This flexibility is what makes Azure a leading platform for modern, data-driven cloud applications.

Chapter 3: Designing for Scalability

Vertical vs. Horizontal Scaling

Scalability is at the core of modern cloud-native architecture. In Azure, designing for scalability is not only a matter of provisioning more compute resources but also about how those resources are organized and consumed under varying loads. Two foundational concepts in scalability—**vertical scaling** and **horizontal scaling**—represent fundamentally different approaches to growing an application's capacity and performance.

Choosing between vertical and horizontal scaling—or more often, strategically combining both—is a critical architectural decision. Each has its own advantages, limitations, and implications for cost, availability, and maintainability.

Understanding Vertical Scaling

Vertical scaling, also known as **scaling up**, refers to increasing the capacity of an existing system by adding more resources—such as CPU, RAM, or storage—to a single instance. In Azure, this might mean resizing a virtual machine (VM), upgrading a database tier, or increasing the performance level of an App Service Plan.

Examples in Azure:

- Upgrading from a B-series VM to a D-series or E-series VM.
- Moving from a Basic to a Premium tier in Azure SQL Database.
- Increasing the compute size in an App Service from P1v2 to P3v2.

```
# Resize a VM to a higher SKU
az vm resize \
  --resource-group myResourceGroup \
  --name myVM \
  --size Standard_D8s_v3
```

Advantages of Vertical Scaling:

- **Simplicity**: Easier to implement with minimal architectural change.
- **Lower latency**: Eliminates inter-process communication between distributed components.
- **Good for legacy apps**: Many monolithic applications are not designed to scale out.

Limitations:

- **Finite limits**: There is always a maximum VM size or service tier.

- **Downtime risk**: Resizing may require restarts or redeployment.

- **Single point of failure**: No redundancy unless additional HA strategies are used.

Vertical scaling is most effective when workloads are tightly coupled, or where the app logic cannot be easily distributed. However, for modern applications expecting high traffic growth, it often becomes a bottleneck.

Understanding Horizontal Scaling

Horizontal scaling, also known as **scaling out**, increases capacity by adding more instances of a service or component. These instances share the workload through load balancing or parallel processing, enabling high availability and elasticity.

In Azure, horizontal scaling is supported by almost all compute services, including:

- Azure Virtual Machine Scale Sets (VMSS)

- Azure App Service Auto-scaling

- Azure Kubernetes Service (AKS) with Horizontal Pod Autoscaler

- Azure Functions with serverless scaling

```
# Enable autoscaling for an App Service Plan
az monitor autoscale create \
  --resource-group myResourceGroup \
  --resource myAppServicePlan \
  --resource-type Microsoft.Web/serverfarms \
  --name autoScaleSettings \
  --min-count 2 \
  --max-count 10 \
  --count 2
```

Advantages of Horizontal Scaling:

- **Elasticity**: Adjusts to traffic spikes automatically.

- **Fault tolerance**: Failure of one instance does not bring down the service.

- **Parallelism**: Better suited to stateless workloads that can run concurrently.

Limitations:

- **Complexity**: Requires architecture that supports concurrency and distributed state management.

- **Data consistency**: Ensuring synchronization across instances can be challenging.

- **Higher initial cost**: May require orchestration (e.g., Kubernetes) or advanced routing logic.

Horizontal scaling is ideal for cloud-native, stateless applications such as microservices, REST APIs, and distributed data processing systems.

Comparing Vertical and Horizontal Scaling

Feature	Vertical Scaling	Horizontal Scaling
Mechanism	Add more power to one machine	Add more machines/instances
Limits	Physical/virtual hardware limits	Practically limitless
Complexity	Low (configuration-level)	High (requires distributed systems)
Downtime risk	Moderate	Low (no need to restart entire app)
Use case suitability	Legacy apps, databases	Web apps, APIs, microservices
Cost model	Pay for larger SKU	Pay for more instances
Availability	Lower unless redundant	Higher by design

Modern Azure-based applications typically combine both strategies for optimal performance and resiliency. For example, a high-performance Azure SQL database (scaled vertically) may serve horizontally scaled microservices running in Azure Kubernetes Service.

Design Principles for Horizontal Scaling

Designing applications to scale horizontally requires architectural practices that support distribution, concurrency, and fault tolerance.

Statelessness

One of the most critical enablers of horizontal scaling is **stateless design**. Stateless services do not store user sessions, cache, or context within the service instance. Instead, they externalize state using:

- Azure   Redis   Cache
- Azure   Cosmos   DB
- Azure   Blob/Table   Storage

This allows any instance to handle any request, enabling load balancing and auto-scaling without conflicts.

Load Balancing

Horizontally scaled applications rely on load balancers to distribute traffic. Azure provides:

- Azure   Load   Balancer   (TCP/UDP)
- Azure   Application   Gateway   (HTTP/HTTPS   +   WAF)
- Azure   Front   Door   (global   layer   7)
- Azure   Traffic   Manager   (DNS-based   routing)

Each of these supports different layers of traffic distribution and works in tandem with scaling policies.

Auto-scaling

Auto-scaling ensures that applications scale automatically based on usage metrics such as CPU, memory, or queue length. Azure services like VM Scale Sets, App Services, and AKS support rule-based or predictive auto-scaling.

```
# Add a rule to scale out when CPU > 75%
az monitor autoscale rule create \
 --resource-group myResourceGroup \
 --autoscale-name autoScaleSettings \
 --condition "Percentage CPU > 75 avg 5m" \
 --scale out 1
```

Decoupling and Asynchronous Messaging

Horizontal scaling thrives when components are **loosely coupled**. Messaging systems like:

- Azure   Service   Bus

- Azure Queue Storage

- Azure Event Grid

help offload work asynchronously, reducing coupling and increasing throughput.

For example, a payment processing API may scale out while offloading receipt generation to a background worker queue.

Partitioning and Sharding

For both compute and data, partitioning ensures even distribution of load:

- **Sharding databases** based on tenant ID or region.

- **Partitioning queues** or event streams by topic or service.

- **Using multiple scale units** in the application layer.

Cosmos DB and SQL Hyperscale both support automatic partitioning at the storage layer.

Hybrid Scaling Approaches

Many systems require a blend of vertical and horizontal strategies:

- **Scale up** to meet immediate short-term demand.

- **Scale out** to support elasticity and redundancy long-term.

For example:

- A backend worker runs on a D8s_v4 VM (vertically scaled).

- The API gateway and frontend scale out across AKS pods (horizontally scaled).

This hybrid approach balances simplicity, performance, and cost.

Monitoring and Observability

Scaling decisions—especially automated ones—must be backed by reliable observability. Use:

- **Azure Monitor** for metrics (CPU, memory, requests)

- **Application Insights** for telemetry and custom metrics

- **Log Analytics** for querying system behavior

- **Azure Advisor** for optimization recommendations

Monitoring allows fine-tuning of scale thresholds and ensures scaling is efficient rather than wasteful.

Cost Considerations

Scaling vertically increases **cost per instance**. Scaling horizontally increases the **number of instances**. Use Azure Cost Management to compare and analyze trade-offs.

Right-sizing tools and budget alerts can prevent over-scaling, and Reserved Instances can offset the cost of base workloads.

Conclusion

Choosing between vertical and horizontal scaling is not binary—it's contextual. The nature of your application, expected traffic patterns, resilience requirements, and budget constraints all influence your strategy.

In Azure, both approaches are well-supported across services. The key is designing applications that are flexible, observable, and adaptable to change. Statelessness, automation, load balancing, and decoupling are foundational patterns that enable intelligent scaling and performance optimization.

By embracing these principles, architects can build systems that not only meet today's needs but gracefully scale into the demands of tomorrow.

Load Balancing Strategies

As applications grow in complexity and scale, managing how user requests and internal traffic are distributed becomes critical. **Load balancing** is a core architectural principle that ensures even distribution of network or application traffic across multiple servers or services. It improves availability, performance, scalability, and fault tolerance. In Azure, load balancing is supported across several layers of the OSI model, enabling both network-level and application-level traffic management.

This section explores essential load balancing strategies, services provided by Azure, design considerations, and implementation best practices for cloud-native applications.

The Purpose of Load Balancing

Load balancing helps solve multiple challenges:

- **Distributes load** to prevent any single instance from becoming a bottleneck.

- **Increases availability** by rerouting traffic when nodes fail.

- **Enhances scalability** by enabling horizontal scaling.

- **Improves performance** with geo-routing and caching.

- **Supports blue-green and canary deployments** for smoother releases.

Effective load balancing strategies ensure optimal resource utilization and better user experience across distributed systems.

Key Load Balancing Methods

There are several algorithms commonly used in load balancing:

- **Round Robin**: Each request is sent to the next server in line.

- **Least Connections**: New requests go to the server with the fewest active connections.

- **IP Hash**: The client's IP determines the server used, enabling session stickiness.

- **Weighted Round Robin / Least Connections**: Assigns more traffic to powerful servers.

- **Random**: Distributes traffic randomly across nodes.

- **Latency-based**: Routes traffic to the endpoint with the lowest latency (used in geo-balancing).

The method chosen affects performance, consistency, and fault tolerance, depending on your application architecture.

Azure Load Balancing Services Overview

Azure provides several load balancing services, each targeting a specific layer of traffic management:

Service	Layer	Scope	Use Case Example
Azure Load Balancer	4	Regional	Distribute TCP/UDP traffic across VMs
Azure Application Gateway	7	Regional	Web app routing, SSL offload, path-based routing

Azure Front Door	7	Global	Global web apps, CDN, WAF, latency-based routing
Azure Traffic Manager	DNS	Global	DNS-based routing to regional endpoints
Azure Kubernetes Service	4/7	Cluster-wide	Load balancing for services in Kubernetes

Each service is designed for specific scenarios. Combining them often results in highly resilient and optimized architectures.

Azure Load Balancer (Layer 4)

Azure Load Balancer is used to distribute TCP and UDP traffic across virtual machines or scale sets. It supports inbound and outbound rules, NAT, and health probes.

Key Features:

- Supports internal and public load balancing.

- Operates at OSI Layer 4 using IP and port-based routing.

- Health probes for failover.

- Supports HA Ports and Zone Redundancy.

```
# Create a Standard Load Balancer with backend pool
az network lb create \
  --name myLoadBalancer \
  --resource-group myResourceGroup \
  --sku Standard \
  --frontend-ip-name myFrontEnd \
  --backend-pool-name myBackEndPool \
  --public-ip-address myPublicIP
```

Azure Load Balancer is best for internal applications or network-based routing (e.g., VPN, RDP access, game servers).

Azure Application Gateway (Layer 7)

Azure Application Gateway is an application-level (Layer 7) load balancer designed for HTTP and HTTPS traffic. It includes features like:

- Path-based routing (e.g., /api goes to backend A, /images to backend B)

- Host-based routing (different domains to different services)

- SSL termination

- Web Application Firewall (WAF)

```
# Add a routing rule to Application Gateway
az network application-gateway url-path-map rule create \
 --gateway-name myAppGateway \
 --resource-group myResourceGroup \
 --path-map-name myPathMap \
 --name myRule \
 --paths /images/* \
 --backend-pool myImageBackendPool \
 --backend-http-settings myHttpSetting
```

This is ideal for web applications, APIs, and microservices requiring security and content-based routing.

Azure Front Door

Azure Front Door is a global, edge-based HTTP/HTTPS load balancer. It routes traffic to the nearest available backend and supports:

- Dynamic site acceleration

- Caching at edge nodes

- SSL offloading

- WAF at the edge

- URL rewriting and redirection

- Priority, performance, or weighted routing

Front Door is the preferred choice for applications with global user bases needing low latency and high availability.

```
# Create a Front Door profile
az network front-door create \
  --resource-group myResourceGroup \
  --name myFrontDoor \
  --accepted-protocols Http Https \
  --backend-address myapp.azurewebsites.net
```

It is often paired with regional Application Gateways for secure, low-latency web delivery.

Azure Traffic Manager (DNS-Based)

Traffic Manager uses DNS to direct clients to specific endpoints based on policies. It works across regions and cloud providers.

Routing methods include:

- **Priority** (failover)

- **Weighted** (A/B testing)

- **Performance** (latency)

- **Geographic** (compliance)

Since it uses DNS, it does not directly route the traffic but guides the client to the endpoint to connect to.

```
# Create a Traffic Manager profile with performance routing
az network traffic-manager profile create \
  --name myTrafficProfile \
  --resource-group myResourceGroup \
  --routing-method Performance \
  --unique-dns-name mytrafficapp \
  --ttl 30 \
  --monitor-protocol HTTP \
  --monitor-port 80 \
  --monitor-path /
```

Combine Traffic Manager with Front Door or Application Gateway to achieve global failover and compliance routing.

Load Balancing in Azure Kubernetes Service (AKS)

In AKS, load balancing is handled through Kubernetes-native services:

- **ClusterIP** (internal cluster traffic)

- **NodePort** (exposes service on each node's IP)

- **LoadBalancer** (provisions Azure Load Balancer)

- **Ingress Controller** (HTTP routing via NGINX, Application Gateway, or Traefik)

Example of an Ingress resource:

```
apiVersion: networking.k8s.io/v1
kind: Ingress
metadata:
 name: web-ingress
 annotations:
  nginx.ingress.kubernetes.io/rewrite-target: /
spec:
 rules:
  - host: app.mydomain.com
   http:
    paths:
     - path: /
      pathType: Prefix
      backend:
       service:
        name: web-service
        port:
         number: 80
```

Kubernetes supports autoscaling and rolling updates, and load balancing helps distribute load effectively across pods.

Load Balancing Patterns

When implementing load balancing in Azure, consider these common patterns:

- **Frontend-Backend Split**: Use Front Door to load balance between Application Gateways or App Services in different regions.

- **Blue-Green Deployments**: Use Traffic Manager or Front Door with weighted routing to test new versions with a subset of traffic.

- **API Gateway + Microservices**: Use Application Gateway or API Management to load balance and secure API requests to containerized or serverless microservices.

- **Multi-Region Redundancy**: Traffic Manager for regional failover combined with Front Door for performance-based routing.

Monitoring and Observability

Azure offers robust tools to monitor load balancing health and effectiveness:

- **Azure Monitor**: Collect metrics on backend health, request count, response times.

- **Network Watcher**: Analyze network flows, diagnose connectivity issues.

- **Application Insights**: Track application-level performance across endpoints.

- **Log Analytics**: Create dashboards for error rates, traffic distribution, regional trends.

Use alerts to proactively scale, shift traffic, or initiate failover based on defined thresholds.

Security Considerations

Securing your load balancers is essential:

- Use **Web Application Firewall (WAF)** in Application Gateway or Front Door.

- Enable **HTTPS** with proper TLS termination.

- Integrate with **Azure DDoS Protection** and **NSGs**.

- Enforce **Access Restrictions** based on IP, headers, or geolocation.

- Use **Private Endpoints** for internal-only routing.

Cost Optimization

Load balancing services vary in cost models:

- Azure Load Balancer: per rule and data processed.

- Application Gateway: per-hour and per-GB processed.

- Front Door: based on routing rules and edge processing.

- Traffic Manager: based on DNS queries.

Optimize by:

- Combining services strategically (e.g., Front Door for public + internal AGW).

- Disabling unused listeners and probes.

- Using standard SKUs for lower cost at scale.

Conclusion

Load balancing is fundamental to high-performing, scalable, and resilient applications in Azure. By understanding the different services—each with their scope, strengths, and limitations—you can design network and application architectures that remain responsive under load, recover quickly from failure, and provide optimal experiences to users around the globe.

Strategically applying these tools ensures that no single component becomes a bottleneck or single point of failure, allowing your architecture to scale intelligently and perform consistently in a cloud-first world.

Auto-scaling in Azure

Auto-scaling is a critical capability for modern applications, enabling systems to automatically adjust their resource allocation based on demand. In Microsoft Azure, auto-scaling ensures applications stay responsive and cost-efficient by scaling out during peak traffic and scaling in during idle periods. Whether you're running virtual machines, web apps, containers, or serverless functions, Azure provides a range of tools and services to implement intelligent, responsive auto-scaling.

This section explores the concept of auto-scaling, the different mechanisms available in Azure, service-specific implementations, policies, best practices, and real-world patterns that help build resilient, scalable cloud-native systems.

What is Auto-scaling?

Auto-scaling refers to the ability of a system to automatically increase or decrease compute capacity to match workload demands without manual intervention.

Auto-scaling can take two main forms:

- **Horizontal scaling**: Adding or removing instances (e.g., VMs, containers, function executions).

- **Vertical scaling**: Increasing or decreasing the size of individual resources (less common   for   automatic   operations).

In most Azure services, auto-scaling focuses on horizontal scaling, which provides greater flexibility, fault tolerance, and scalability.

Benefits of Auto-scaling

- **Cost   efficiency**:   Pay   only   for   the   resources   you   need.

- **Performance   optimization**:   Maintain   responsiveness   under   varying   load.

- **High   availability**:   Reduce   the   risk   of   overload-related   failures.

- **Operational simplicity**: Reduces the need for manual scaling and monitoring.

Azure Auto-scaling Tools and Services

Azure offers built-in auto-scaling capabilities across a variety of services:

Azure Service	Auto-scaling Support
Virtual Machine Scale Sets	Rule-based, metric-based
App Services	CPU/memory/queue-based
Azure Kubernetes Service (AKS)	Cluster and pod autoscaling
Azure Functions	Event-driven scaling
Azure Logic Apps	Automatic parallelism
Azure SQL Database (Hyperscale)	Automatic storage scaling
Azure Cosmos DB	Throughput (RU/s) scaling

Each service offers different levels of customization, metrics, and control over how scaling occurs.

Auto-scaling Virtual Machine Scale Sets (VMSS)

Azure VM Scale Sets allow you to create and manage a group of load-balanced VMs. You can define auto-scaling rules based on metrics such as CPU usage, memory pressure, or custom metrics through Azure Monitor.

```
# Enable autoscale for a scale set
az monitor autoscale create \
  --resource-group myResourceGroup \
  --resource myScaleSet \
  --resource-type Microsoft.Compute/virtualMachineScaleSets \
  --name autoscaleSetting \
  --min-count 2 \
  --max-count 10 \
  --count 2
```

```
# Add a rule to scale out when CPU > 75%
az monitor autoscale rule create \
  --resource-group myResourceGroup \
  --autoscale-name autoscaleSetting \
  --condition "Percentage CPU > 75 avg 5m" \
  --scale out 1
```

Considerations:

- VMs take time to start; build rules with delay in mind.

- Use **Custom Script Extensions** or **Desired State Configuration (DSC)** to prepare VMs at scale.

- Use Application Gateway or Load Balancer to route traffic.

Auto-scaling Azure App Services

App Services offer native auto-scaling based on built-in or custom metrics, including:

- CPU or memory percentage

- Request count

- Queue length in Azure Storage or Service Bus

- Custom Azure Monitor metrics

Auto-scaling is configured through **App Service Plans** and managed using **Autoscale Settings**.

```
# Basic auto-scale setup for App Services
az monitor autoscale create \
  --resource-group myResourceGroup \
  --resource myAppServicePlan \
  --resource-type Microsoft.Web/serverfarms \
  --name autoscaleSetting \
  --min-count 1 \
  --max-count 5 \
  --count 1
```

Custom rules allow developers to respond to business-specific metrics (e.g., orders per minute, session duration, etc.), improving precision.

Auto-scaling in Azure Kubernetes Service (AKS)

AKS supports two forms of auto-scaling:

- **Cluster Autoscaler**: Adjusts the number of VM nodes in the cluster.

- **Horizontal Pod Autoscaler (HPA)**: Adjusts the number of pod replicas for a deployment.

```
# Enable HPA for a deployment
kubectl autoscale deployment myapp \
  --cpu-percent=50 \
  --min=2 \
  --max=10
```

HPA works by monitoring pod metrics like CPU or memory. Cluster Autoscaler works at the infrastructure level, adding/removing VMs based on pending pods.

Best Practices:

- Use **metrics-server** in AKS for accurate pod-level metrics.

- Combine with custom metrics adapters for advanced telemetry.

- Tune cooldown and stabilization windows to prevent flapping.

Auto-scaling Serverless: Azure Functions

Azure Functions use a **consumption plan**, which automatically scales based on event triggers. It's the most elastic model available—functions can scale from zero to thousands of concurrent executions nearly instantly.

Key triggers include:

- HTTP   requests

- Queue   messages

- Blob   storage   events

- Event   Hubs,   Service   Bus

Scaling is driven by **event volume** and **processing duration**.

```json
# Sample function configuration in function.json
{
  "bindings": [
    {
      "name": "myQueueItem",
      "type": "queueTrigger",
      "direction": "in",
      "queueName": "myqueue-items",
      "connection": "AzureWebJobsStorage"
    }
  ]
}
```

Premium Plans and **Dedicated Plans** allow for pre-warmed instances, better suited for latency-sensitive workloads.

Custom Auto-scaling with Azure Monitor

In addition to service-specific settings, **Azure Monitor Autoscale** allows you to define custom rules for nearly any resource.

You can scale based on:

- CPU, memory
- Disk I/O
- Custom log metrics (e.g., number of 500 errors)
- Application Insights metrics

You can also use **webhooks** to integrate auto-scaling with third-party systems or initiate external processes.

```json
# Example of webhook-based custom scale trigger
{
  "location": "East US",
  "properties": {
    "enabled": true,
    "targetResourceUri": "/subscriptions/.../resourceGroups/.../providers/Microsoft.Web/serverfarms/myAppServicePlan",
    "profiles": [
```

```
{
  "name": "scaleProfile",
  "capacity": {
    "minimum": "1",
    "maximum": "10",
    "default": "1"
  },
  "rules": [
    {
      "metricTrigger": {
        "metricName": "Requests",
        "metricResourceUri": "...",
        "timeGrain": "PT1M",
        "statistic": "Average",
        "timeWindow": "PT5M",
        "timeAggregation": "Average",
        "operator": "GreaterThan",
        "threshold": 1000
      },
      "scaleAction": {
        "direction": "Increase",
        "type": "ChangeCount",
        "value": "1",
        "cooldown": "PT5M"
      }
    }
  ]
}
}
```

Best Practices for Auto-scaling

1. **Design for statelessness**: Stateless services can be scaled freely without coordination   overhead.

2. **Use metrics that reflect real user impact**: Prefer request count, queue length, or custom   KPIs   over   raw   CPU.

3. **Add cooldown periods**: Prevent flapping (rapid scaling up/down) by configuring stabilization   delays.

4. **Test scaling thresholds under load**: Use Azure Load Testing to validate real-world behavior.

5. **Combine auto-scaling with alerts**: Get notified before reaching critical thresholds.

6. **Enable logging and observability**: Use Application Insights and Log Analytics for post-scaling   analysis.

Real-World Use Cases

E-commerce Store

- Auto-scale   frontend   App   Services   based   on   HTTP   request   count.

- Use   HPA   to   scale   backend   microservices   during   product   launches.

- Scale   Cosmos   DB   RU/s   manually   via   API   or   enable   autoscale.

SaaS Application

- Scale App Service plans for multi-tenant APIs based on tenant activity.

- Use separate Function Apps per tenant in Premium plan for isolation.

- Auto-scale   SQL   Elastic   Pools   based   on   DTU   usage.

Streaming and IoT Platform

- Auto-scale Event Hub throughput and Function Apps for data ingestion.

- Use Kubernetes-based processing pipeline with cluster autoscaler and HPA.

- Use   custom   metrics   (messages/sec)   for   scaling   logic.

Conclusion

Auto-scaling in Azure is a powerful feature that enables dynamic application performance tuning without manual intervention. From traditional VM-based workloads to cutting-edge serverless functions, Azure provides mechanisms to adjust compute resources intelligently based on real-time demand.

Designing with auto-scaling in mind encourages modularity, observability, and efficiency. By leveraging Azure's built-in tools and aligning scaling with application behavior and business metrics, architects can create systems that are resilient under pressure, lean in cost, and capable of growing with user demand.

Designing Stateless Services

Stateless services are foundational to scalable, resilient, and cloud-native application architectures. In a distributed system, especially in the cloud, the ability to replicate, restart, or relocate service instances without losing data or functionality is critical. Stateless services make this possible by removing dependencies on local or in-memory state, enabling seamless horizontal scaling, high availability, and easier fault recovery.

In this section, we explore what it means for a service to be stateless, why it's important, how to design stateless services effectively in Azure, and what tools and patterns support statelessness across compute, storage, and networking layers.

What is a Stateless Service?

A **stateless service** does not retain any session information or state data between requests. Each interaction is independent, and any required data must be passed with the request or retrieved from an external store.

In contrast, **stateful services** maintain context—such as user sessions, transactions, or cached data—within the process or memory of a particular server instance.

Statelessness simplifies service replication and failover because any instance of the service can handle any request at any time.

Examples of Stateless Services:

- RESTful   APIs

- Azure   Functions

- Azure   App   Services   with   token-based   authentication

- Microservices   using   external   databases   or   caches

Why Statelessness Matters

Scalability

Stateless services can be scaled horizontally without coordination. This makes them ideal for use with load balancers, autoscaling groups, and Kubernetes.

Resilience

If an instance fails, another can immediately take its place without losing data. There's no dependency on restoring in-memory state.

Simplified Deployment

Stateless services can be deployed, upgraded, and rolled back independently. There's no need to worry about session persistence or in-memory synchronization.

Cost Efficiency

Since stateless services can be stopped and started freely, they align well with consumption-based billing models like Azure Functions or container orchestrators.

Key Principles of Designing Stateless Services

Externalize All State

All stateful information should reside in external systems:

- **Databases** for persistent data (Azure SQL, Cosmos DB, PostgreSQL)

- **Blob** or **File** **Storage** for files and binary objects

- **Redis** **Cache** for temporary or session data

- **Queues** and **Event** **Hubs** for message handling

This allows service instances to be disposable and interchangeable.

Idempotency

Stateless services should be **idempotent**—repeating a request with the same input should produce the same result. This is especially important in distributed systems where retries and network errors are common.

```
POST /payment/charge/12345
{
  "amount": 100,
  "currency": "USD"
}
```

Ensure the server tracks the request ID (e.g., 12345) and doesn't double-charge on retries.

Token-based Authentication

Session state for user authentication should not be stored server-side. Instead, use:

- **JWT (JSON Web Tokens)**
- **OAuth 2.0 bearer tokens**
- **Azure Active Directory access tokens**

These tokens carry all necessary user information and can be validated independently on each request.

Dependency Injection and Configuration Management

Avoid hard-coded logic or environmental assumptions. Use Azure App Configuration or environment variables to externalize configuration so services remain flexible and consistent across environments.

Stateless Architecture Patterns in Azure

Azure App Services

App Services are inherently stateless. When an instance restarts or scales, session state is not preserved. Store user sessions in:

- Azure Redis Cache
- Azure SQL Database
- Cosmos DB

Use deployment slots for zero-downtime deployments and avoid in-memory session state.

Azure Functions

Functions are ephemeral. They can start and stop at any time and across any region. Stateless logic is required to ensure they behave reliably:

- Pass context in the function trigger (e.g., message body)
- Store durable information externally
- Use Durable Functions for orchestrated workflows

Azure Kubernetes Service (AKS)

In AKS, pods are scheduled dynamically, and workloads may shift across nodes. Stateless microservices can be easily distributed and autoscaled using:

- Deployments   with   replicas

- Services   with   selectors

- Ingress   with   round-robin   routing

Use ConfigMaps and Secrets for dynamic configuration and credentials.

Event-Driven Systems

Design services to be triggered by events and handle them independently:

- Azure   Event   Grid

- Azure   Service   Bus

- Azure   Event   Hubs

Ensure services process events idempotently and use poison message handling strategies for failures.

Building Resilient Stateless APIs

APIs are a natural fit for stateless design. Here's how to ensure they remain robust and scalable:

Use RESTful Design

Structure endpoints using nouns and HTTP verbs. Ensure each call is independent and complete.

```
GET /users/12345
POST /orders
PUT /profile/12345
```

Stateless Authentication

Use OAuth 2.0, Azure AD B2C, or Managed Identity to issue bearer tokens. Avoid server-side session storage.

```
Authorization: Bearer eyJhbGciOiJIUzI1...
```

Retry and Circuit Breaker Patterns

Use libraries like Polly in .NET to implement:

- Retry with exponential backoff

- Timeout handling

- Circuit breakers for failing dependencies

```
var retryPolicy = Policy
  .Handle<HttpRequestException>()
  .WaitAndRetryAsync(3,    retryAttempt    =>    TimeSpan.FromSeconds(Math.Pow(2,
retryAttempt)));
```

These patterns ensure resiliency in stateless services when dependent services experience transient failures.

State Management in Stateless Systems

While services themselves should be stateless, managing **application state** remains essential. The key is **where** and **how** the state is stored.

Session State

Move session data to centralized stores:

- **Azure Redis Cache** for low-latency reads/writes

- **Cosmos DB** for globally distributed access

- **Table Storage** for simple key-value session data

Application State

Application-level state such as orders, profiles, logs, and preferences should be stored in:

- Relational DBs for structured data (Azure SQL, PostgreSQL)

- NoSQL stores for high-volume data (Cosmos DB)

Use access patterns that match the data structure and ensure consistency models align with business needs.

Durable State (Workflows)

For orchestrated, long-running workflows, use:

- **Durable Functions** with Azure Storage
- **Logic Apps** with stateful execution

These handle checkpoints, retries, and state progression while keeping the service logic stateless.

Monitoring Stateless Services

Even though stateless services are ephemeral, observability must be persistent:

- **Use Application Insights** to collect request traces, exceptions, and dependencies.
- **Log correlation IDs** for tracing across distributed components.
- **Emit custom metrics** for rate, error, duration (RED model).
- **Use distributed tracing** with OpenTelemetry for end-to-end visibility.

Instrumentation should be decoupled from the service logic to ensure minimal overhead and vendor portability.

Challenges and Mitigations

Challenge	Mitigation Strategy
Handling retries and duplicates	Implement idempotency
Managing session state	Externalize to Redis or Cosmos DB
Debugging failures in ephemeral systems	Use distributed tracing and centralized logs
Config and secret management	Use Azure Key Vault and App Configuration
Cross-service data consistency	Use event sourcing, compensating transactions

Stateless services simplify horizontal scaling but require intentional design to ensure reliability and data integrity in distributed environments.

Conclusion

Designing stateless services is not merely a technical choice—it's an architectural philosophy that aligns perfectly with cloud-native principles. In Azure, statelessness unlocks the full potential of platform elasticity, enabling services to scale, failover, and recover with minimal operational overhead.

By externalizing state, embracing idempotency, leveraging Azure-native patterns and tools, and building with resilience in mind, architects and developers can craft services that are truly ready for global, mission-critical workloads. Stateless services are not only the foundation for scalability—they are the blueprint for sustainable growth and operational excellence in the cloud.

Chapter 4: High Availability and Disaster Recovery

Azure Regions and Availability Zones

Building highly available systems is essential for any modern application architecture. In Microsoft Azure, achieving high availability begins with a deep understanding of its **regional infrastructure model**, including **Azure Regions**, **Availability Zones**, and **paired regions**. These foundational constructs enable architects to design solutions that are fault-tolerant, resilient to data center failures, and capable of seamless disaster recovery.

This section explores the geographical and structural elements of Azure's infrastructure and how they can be leveraged to build high-availability solutions that meet uptime SLAs and regulatory requirements.

Azure Regions: The Foundation of Global Distribution

An **Azure Region** is a set of datacenters deployed within a specific geographic area, connected through a low-latency network. Each region is designed to be independent and isolated from other regions to ensure fault isolation and data sovereignty.

As of writing, Azure spans over **60+ regions** globally—more than any other cloud provider. This vast presence supports global applications and region-specific compliance requirements.

Examples of Azure Regions:

- East   US

- West   Europe

- Southeast   Asia

- Australia   Central

- Japan   East

- South   Africa   North

Azure Regions are chosen based on:

- Proximity   to   end   users   (latency)

- Data   residency   requirements   (GDPR,   HIPAA)

- Regulatory   compliance   (FedRAMP,   ISO,   CJIS)

- Redundancy   and   failover   planning

```
# List available regions using Azure CLI
az account list-locations --output table
```

When deploying a new resource in Azure, choosing the right region impacts everything from performance to compliance.

Availability Zones: Fault Isolation Within a Region

Availability Zones (AZs) are physically separate datacenters within a single Azure region. Each zone has its own power, cooling, and networking infrastructure, designed to protect applications from datacenter-level failures.

Azure guarantees **99.99% uptime SLA** for resources deployed across multiple Availability Zones.

Each region with AZs typically has **three zones.** You can use them for:

- Deploying   redundant   compute   instances   (VMs,   AKS   nodes)

- Zone-redundant   storage   (ZRS)

- Load-balanced   applications

Services That Support Availability Zones:

- Azure   Virtual   Machines

- Azure   Kubernetes   Service   (AKS)

- Azure   App   Services   (Premium   v3)

- Azure   SQL   Database   (Zone-redundant   configuration)

- Azure   Load   Balancer   (Standard)

- Azure   VPN   Gateway   (Zone-redundant   SKU)

```
# Create a zonal VM
az vm create \
```

```
--resource-group myResourceGroup \
--name myZonalVM \
--image UbuntuLTS \
--size Standard_DS1_v2 \
--zone 2
```

Zonal vs. Zone-redundant Resources:

- **Zonal**: Pinned to a specific zone (e.g., VM in Zone 1).

- **Zone-redundant**: Spanned across multiple zones (e.g., ZRS storage).

Region Pairs: Planning for Disaster Recovery

Each Azure region is **paired** with another region within the same geography to support data replication and recovery. This is known as a **region pair**.

For example:

- East   US   ↔   West   US

- North   Europe   ↔   West   Europe

- Southeast   Asia   ↔   East   Asia

Benefits of Region Pairs:

- At   least   300   miles   apart   (where   possible)

- Data   replication   for   geo-redundant   services   (e.g.,   GRS   storage)

- Platform   updates   are   rolled   out   sequentially   to   minimize   risk

- Prioritized   recovery   during   widespread   outages

When designing disaster recovery (DR) solutions, region pairs offer a best practice foundation for **geo-redundancy**.

Designing Applications Across Regions and Zones

Single Region, Multi-Zone

- Suitable for high availability within a geographic boundary.
- Protects against single datacenter failures.
- Common for business-critical apps not subject to geo-redundancy needs.

Example Architecture:

- Azure Load Balancer with VMs in Zones 1, 2, and 3.
- Zone-redundant Azure SQL or Cosmos DB.
- ZRS (zone-redundant storage) for high durability.

Multi-Region Deployment

- Ensures resilience in case of entire region outage.
- Supports business continuity and compliance.
- Requires traffic routing (Traffic Manager, Front Door) and data replication.

Example Architecture:

- Azure Front Door distributes traffic between East US and Central US.
- Cosmos DB with multi-region writes.
- Azure SQL with geo-replication.
- Application Gateway or Azure App Services deployed in both regions.

High Availability Design Considerations

When using Azure regions and zones, the following principles ensure robust HA designs:

Redundancy

Deploy multiple instances of components across zones or regions:

- Load-balanced frontends

- Replicated data stores
- Backup services and vaults

Failover

Build in automatic and manual failover capabilities:

- Use Azure Traffic Manager or Front Door for DNS-based routing.
- Monitor health and implement rules for failover switching.
- Design apps to handle service unavailability gracefully.

Latency Awareness

Minimize user-perceived latency by routing requests to the closest healthy region:

- Front Door supports performance-based routing.
- Cosmos DB ensures local reads with multi-region configuration.

State Management

Store application state in zone-redundant or geo-redundant services:

- Azure Blob Storage with GRS or RA-GRS
- Azure SQL Geo-Replication
- Cosmos DB Multi-region Writes

Avoid dependencies on in-memory or local disk-based state.

Compliance and Data Residency

Azure enables organizations to meet data residency regulations by:

- Offering sovereign clouds (e.g., Azure Government, Azure China)
- Keeping customer data within selected regions
- Providing region-based access controls and policies

Use **Azure Policy** to enforce deployment only within allowed regions:

```
{
  "if": {
    "not": {
      "field": "location",
      "in": ["eastus", "westus"]
    }
  },
  "then": {
    "effect": "deny"
  }
}
```

Monitoring Availability

Visibility into service health is essential for HA design:

- Use **Azure Monitor** and **Log Analytics** for telemetry.
- Configure **Application Insights** to detect anomalies.
- Set up **Health Probes** for load balancers.
- Use **Service Health Alerts** to stay informed of Azure-wide incidents.

Azure also provides a **Service Health Dashboard** for tracking region-specific service issues.

Real-World Scenarios

SaaS Platform with Global Customers

- Front Door routes users to the nearest regional deployment.
- App Services and Cosmos DB deployed in East US and West Europe.
- Traffic Manager switches traffic if a region becomes unavailable.
- Geo-redundant backups in paired regions ensure data safety.

Healthcare System with Compliance Requirements

- All patient data stored in a single Azure region (e.g., Canada Central).

- Services deployed across Availability Zones for HA.

- Azure SQL with Zone-redundant configuration.

- Azure Policy ensures deployments only within the region.

Enterprise Analytics Platform

- Ingests IoT data into Azure Event Hubs with ZRS.

- Processes data with Azure Functions across zones.

- Stores results in Azure Synapse Analytics with geo-backup enabled.

- Dashboard access via Front Door with traffic routing between region pairs.

Conclusion

High availability starts with sound architectural choices at the infrastructure level. Azure's global network of regions and datacenter zones empowers architects to design applications that remain accessible, resilient, and performant—even during localized or widespread outages.

By understanding and leveraging Azure Regions, Availability Zones, and region pairs, you can meet strict uptime SLAs, regulatory demands, and user expectations with confidence. In the next sections, we'll examine redundancy techniques, backup strategies, and complete disaster recovery planning that build upon this solid infrastructure foundation.

Redundancy and Replication Techniques

Redundancy and replication are foundational principles in designing highly available and fault-tolerant systems. In Azure, these techniques help ensure that applications remain operational even when components fail, infrastructure becomes unavailable, or regions experience outages. By strategically duplicating workloads and synchronizing data across services, zones, or regions, architects can build resilient systems that meet stringent availability SLAs and compliance standards.

This section explores the various redundancy and replication mechanisms available across Azure services and how to use them effectively in production architectures.

Understanding Redundancy

Redundancy is the duplication of critical components or functions of a system to increase reliability and availability. Redundancy can be implemented at multiple levels:

- **Infrastructure Redundancy**: Multiple VMs, networks, or hardware.

- **Application Redundancy**: Redundant service instances across zones or regions.

- **Data Redundancy**: Replicated data stores to avoid loss in the event of failure.

Azure supports all three categories, and the level of redundancy selected depends on the criticality of the workload.

Understanding Replication

Replication refers to the continuous copying of data from one location to another to ensure consistency and durability. In Azure, replication is typically:

- **Synchronous** (real-time) for low-latency and strong consistency.

- **Asynchronous** for greater distance and minimal performance impact, but eventual consistency.

Replication is central to business continuity, enabling recovery from failures without significant data loss.

Redundancy in Azure Compute Services

Virtual Machines and Availability Sets

An **Availability Set** spreads VMs across multiple **fault domains** (physical racks) and **update domains** (logical groups for patching). This ensures that not all VMs are impacted by hardware failure or maintenance at the same time.

```
# Create an availability set
az vm availability-set create \
  --resource-group myResourceGroup \
  --name myAvailabilitySet \
  --platform-fault-domain-count 2 \
  --platform-update-domain-count 2
```

Use Availability Sets to provide redundancy within a single datacenter.

Virtual Machine Scale Sets (VMSS)

VMSS enable horizontal scaling and redundancy. When combined with **zones**, VM instances can be distributed across multiple Availability Zones for zone redundancy.

```
# Create a VMSS with zonal distribution
az vmss create \
  --resource-group myResourceGroup \
  --name myVMSS \
  --image UbuntuLTS \
  --zones 1 2 3 \
  --upgrade-policy-mode automatic
```

App Services and Zone Redundancy

Premium App Service plans support zone redundancy. For critical apps, use deployment slots for zero-downtime updates and health-based routing.

Replication in Azure Storage

Azure Storage provides multiple redundancy options for blob, table, queue, and file storage:

Replication Type	Description	Redundancy Scope
LRS	Locally Redundant Storage – 3 copies within one datacenter	Intra-region
ZRS	Zone-Redundant Storage – 3 copies across zones in one region	Intra-region
GRS	Geo-Redundant Storage – LRS + async copy to paired region	Cross-region
RA-GRS	Read-Access Geo-Redundant – GRS + read access to secondary	Cross-region
GZRS	Geo-Zone Redundant – ZRS + async copy to paired region	Cross-region
RA-GZRS	GZRS + read access to secondary	Cross-region

```
# Create a GRS storage account
az storage account create \
  --name mystorageacct \
```

```
--resource-group myResourceGroup \
--location eastus \
--sku Standard_GRS \
--kind StorageV2
```

Choose redundancy based on your durability needs and failover strategy. For mission-critical workloads, **RA-GZRS** offers maximum durability and availability.

Replication in Azure Databases

Azure SQL Database

Supports **active geo-replication**, allowing up to four readable secondaries in different regions.

```
# Configure geo-replication
az sql db replica create \
  --name mydb \
  --partner-server mysecondaryserver \
  --resource-group myResourceGroup \
  --server myprimaryserver
```

Also supports **auto-failover groups**, which allow automatic redirection of clients to secondary regions during outages.

Azure Cosmos DB

Cosmos DB provides native, automatic, multi-region replication with configurable **consistency levels**:

- Strong

- Bounded   staleness

- Session

- Consistent   prefix

- Eventual

Supports **multi-master write** configurations, ensuring high availability and low latency globally.

```
# Enable multi-region replication
```

```
az cosmosdb update \
  --name myCosmosAccount \
  --resource-group myResourceGroup \
  --locations regionName=eastus failoverPriority=0 \
  --locations regionName=westeurope failoverPriority=1
```

Azure Database for PostgreSQL / MySQL

Flexible Server supports **read replicas** within the same region. Upcoming features include cross-region replicas for DR.

Redundancy in Networking

Load Balancing Across Zones

Azure Load Balancer and **Application Gateway** can be deployed across zones to ensure connectivity even if one zone fails.

```
# Create a zone-redundant public load balancer
az network lb create \
  --resource-group myResourceGroup \
  --name myLoadBalancer \
  --sku Standard \
  --frontend-ip-name myFrontend \
  --backend-pool-name myBackend \
  --public-ip-address myPublicIP \
  --zones 1 2 3
```

DNS-Level Redundancy with Traffic Manager

Azure Traffic Manager provides DNS-based failover and geographic routing, making it suitable for cross-region redundancy.

- **Priority routing** ensures failover from primary to secondary.
- **Performance routing** routes users to the lowest-latency region.
- **Geographic routing** supports compliance and data residency.

Redundancy in Messaging and Event Systems

Azure Service Bus

Premium tier supports **zone redundancy**. Messages are replicated across zones automatically, ensuring delivery even if a zone goes offline.

Azure Event Hubs

Supports **availability zones** in select regions. Provides message durability with internal replication and data retention settings.

Azure Queue Storage

Backed by Azure Storage, benefits from the same redundancy options (LRS, GRS, ZRS, etc.).

Resilience Patterns Using Redundancy

Active-Active Deployment

Both regions or zones are active and share traffic. Requires data synchronization and conflict resolution logic.

Use Cases:

- Cosmos DB with multi-master writes

- App Services behind Front Door

Active-Passive Deployment

Traffic goes to primary region; passive region is on standby and activated on failure.

Use Cases:

- Azure SQL with auto-failover groups

- Traffic Manager with priority routing

Warm Standby

Reduced version of the app runs in a secondary region, scaled up only during disaster recovery.

Cold Standby

No running resources in secondary until a disaster is declared. Longest recovery time but cost-efficient.

Monitoring Redundant Systems

Use the following to ensure redundancy mechanisms are functioning:

• **Azure**	**Monitor**	for	custom	metrics
• **Log**	**Analytics**	for	health	queries
• **Application**	**Insights**	for	availability	testing
• **Activity**	**Logs**	for	audit	trails
• **Service** **Health**	**Alerts**	for	regional incident	detection

Redundancy is only valuable if actively monitored and validated.

Conclusion

Redundancy and replication are not optional—they are vital for business continuity in the cloud. Azure's extensive suite of zone-redundant, region-replicated, and geo-distributed services allow architects to design applications that continue to operate even under adverse conditions.

By understanding and implementing redundancy at every layer—compute, storage, database, networking, and messaging—you ensure that your architecture is not just scalable but resilient. The right redundancy strategy depends on your recovery time objectives (RTO), recovery point objectives (RPO), and cost constraints. When used wisely, these techniques are the backbone of robust, always-on cloud systems.

Backup and Restore Strategies

Data is the lifeblood of modern digital services, and safeguarding it is paramount. Backups ensure that you can recover from accidental deletions, corruption, malicious attacks, or system failures. In Microsoft Azure, backup and restore are not limited to simple file copies—they encompass entire virtual machines, databases, file systems, application states, and even infrastructure configurations. Robust **backup and restore strategies** are a core component of any cloud architecture aiming to meet business continuity and disaster recovery (BCDR) objectives.

This section provides a comprehensive look at Azure's backup solutions, explores strategic approaches to data protection, and presents real-world implementation best practices for various services.

The Importance of Backup and Restore

Backup is not just a technical task—it is an essential business safeguard. Key reasons for implementing robust strategies include:

- Protection against accidental deletion
- Ransomware and malware recovery
- Compliance with regulatory standards (e.g., GDPR, HIPAA)
- Recovery from infrastructure failure
- Versioning and rollback capabilities

An effective strategy balances **Recovery Point Objective (RPO)** and **Recovery Time Objective (RTO)** while remaining cost-effective.

Azure Backup: The Centralized Backup Platform

Azure Backup is a first-party service that simplifies backup and restore for multiple Azure services and on-premises workloads. It is agent-based and integrates with:

- Azure VMs (Windows/Linux)
- SQL Server in Azure VMs
- Azure Files and Azure Blob Storage
- On-premises servers via Azure Backup Agent or MARS
- Azure Kubernetes Service (preview)

Key Features:

- Long-term retention (up to 10 years)
- Geo-redundant or locally redundant backup storage
- Backup encryption using customer-managed or platform-managed keys
- Centralized monitoring via Azure Monitor
- Application-consistent backups for databases and workloads

```
# Create a Recovery Services vault
az backup vault create \
  --name myRecoveryVault \
  --resource-group myResourceGroup \
  --location eastus
```

Backup Strategy for Azure Virtual Machines

Azure Backup allows **snapshot-based VM backups** with point-in-time restore capabilities. Backups can be scheduled daily or weekly with custom retention policies.

Steps:

1. Create a Recovery Services vault.
2. Register the VM with the vault.
3. Define a backup policy (frequency + retention).
4. Enable backup on the VM.

```
# Enable backup for a VM
az backup protection enable-for-vm \
  --vault-name myRecoveryVault \
  --resource-group myResourceGroup \
  --vm myVM \
  --policy-name DefaultPolicy
```

Restore options:

- Restore the full VM (new instance or replace existing)
- Restore individual files using file recovery script

Best Practices:

- Enable zone-redundant backup storage if supported.
- Use tagging to identify protected resources.
- Regularly test restore procedures.
- Automate policy enforcement via Azure Policy.

Backup Strategies for Azure SQL Database

Azure SQL Database offers **built-in automatic backups** for all service tiers. Backups are stored in **RA-GRS** storage for up to:

- 7–35 days (standard)

- 10 years (Long-term Retention)

No user configuration is needed, but **Long-term Retention (LTR)** must be manually enabled for extended compliance use.

```
# Enable LTR for a database
az sql db ltr-policy set \
  --resource-group myResourceGroup \
  --server mySqlServer \
  --database mydb \
  --weekly-retention P1Y
```

Restore options:

- Point-in-time restore to a new database

- Restore deleted databases within the retention window

- Geo-restore in a different region if the primary is unavailable

Backup for Azure Files and Blob Storage

Azure File Share Backup

- Natively integrated with Azure Backup.

- Application-consistent snapshots are stored in Recovery Services vaults.

- Ideal for legacy applications using SMB shares.

```
# Protect Azure File share
az backup protection enable-for-azurefileshare \
  --vault-name myRecoveryVault \
  --resource-group myResourceGroup \
```

```
--storage-account mystorageacct \
--share-name myshare \
--policy-name DefaultPolicy
```

Azure Blob Storage Backup

Blob storage does not use Azure Backup but offers native redundancy features:

- **Soft Delete** for blobs and containers
- **Blob versioning**
- **Point-in-time restore** for containers
- **Immutable blob storage** for compliance

```
# Enable blob soft delete
az storage blob service-properties delete-policy update \
  --account-name mystorageacct \
  --enable true \
  --days-retained 30
```

Use a combination of snapshots, lifecycle rules, and versioning for full data protection.

Protecting On-Premises Workloads

Azure Backup supports **hybrid environments** through:

- **Microsoft Azure Recovery Services (MARS) Agent**: For file/folder-level backup on Windows servers.
- **System Center DPM** or **Azure Backup Server**: For application-consistent backups of SQL, Exchange, and SharePoint.
- **Azure Arc**: Extends Azure Backup to Arc-enabled servers.

Data is encrypted before transmission and can be stored in GRS or LRS vaults.

Backup for Azure Kubernetes Service (AKS)

AKS does not have native Azure Backup support (as of now), but you can implement protection using:

- **Velero**: Open-source backup/restore for Kubernetes objects and persistent volumes.

- **Azure Disk Snapshots**: Manual or automated snapshots for attached volumes.

- **Azure Backup integration** (preview): Protects entire clusters or selected workloads.

Always back up:

- ConfigMaps and Secrets (or externalize to Azure Key Vault)

- Stateful workloads with persistent volumes

- Helm chart values and deployment manifests

Backup for Azure DevOps and Configuration

Backups go beyond data—they include infrastructure-as-code and configuration:

- Store ARM, Bicep, and Terraform files in Git.

- Use GitHub Actions or Azure Pipelines for version control and rollback.

- Export Azure Policy assignments and role definitions regularly.

- Export and document NSGs, Route Tables, and DNS zones.

Example: Scheduled pipeline to back up Azure Bicep templates and export resources nightly.

Testing Your Restore Plan

A backup is only as good as its **restore**. Regular testing ensures readiness and minimizes RTO in real incidents.

Guidelines:

- Perform test restores in non-production environments.

- Validate data integrity post-restore.

- Document and automate the restore process.

- Include test restores in regular DR drills.

Azure Backup supports **restore-as-job**, which allows isolated testing without disrupting production workloads.

Security and Compliance in Backup

- Encrypt backup data at rest and in transit.

- Use **Customer Managed Keys (CMK)** for enhanced control.

- Apply **Role-Based Access Control (RBAC)** to limit backup access.

- Enable **multi-user authorization** for destructive actions (preview).

- Configure **alerts and notifications** for backup failures.

Azure Backup is **ISO 27001**, **SOC**, **HIPAA**, and **GDPR** compliant, making it suitable for regulated industries.

Cost Management

Backup costs are composed of:

- **Protected instance cost** (based on size)

- **Backup storage cost** (GB/month)

Tips for optimization:

- Use **LRS** where cross-region is not required.

- Prune backup retention policies.

- Use Azure Cost Management to track backup expenditures.

- Tag resources with backup status for better visibility.

Conclusion

Backup and restore strategies are essential for ensuring business continuity, meeting compliance requirements, and protecting critical data. Azure provides a comprehensive suite of backup tools for VMs, databases, files, containers, and on-premises systems. Combined with native features like soft delete, versioning, and snapshots, you can implement a multi-layered data protection strategy.

Architects must consider RTO, RPO, cost, automation, and compliance when designing backup solutions. Ultimately, backup isn't just about data—it's about trust, resilience, and the ability to recover when it matters most.

Disaster Recovery Planning in Azure

Disaster recovery (DR) is a critical component of business continuity that ensures systems can be restored and services resumed following major disruptions such as data center failures, cyberattacks, natural disasters, or accidental data deletion. In Microsoft Azure, disaster recovery planning is about more than just backups—it involves designing systems to be fault-tolerant, geographically redundant, and capable of restoring business functionality with minimal downtime and data loss.

This section explores comprehensive disaster recovery strategies in Azure, the services that support them, common patterns and scenarios, and practical guidance for building resilient systems that can recover quickly and efficiently in the face of disaster.

The Goals of Disaster Recovery

Effective disaster recovery planning should align with two key metrics:

- **Recovery Time Objective (RTO)**: The maximum acceptable time an application or system can be down after a failure.

- **Recovery Point Objective (RPO)**: The maximum acceptable amount of data loss measured in time.

For example, a financial trading platform may require RTO < 5 minutes and RPO < 1 minute, whereas a file archive system may tolerate RTO of several hours.

The DR plan must be tailored to the application's **business criticality**, **compliance requirements**, and **cost tolerance**.

Key Components of a Disaster Recovery Plan

A comprehensive DR plan should address the following:

1. **Inventory of critical workloads and dependencies**

2. **Failover and failback mechanisms**

3. **Replication and data protection strategies**

4. **Automation of recovery processes**

5. **Monitoring, alerting, and testing**

6. **Role assignments and access controls**

7. **Compliance and documentation requirements**

These elements help ensure that every part of the system can be restored systematically and securely.

Azure Site Recovery (ASR)

Azure Site Recovery is Azure's native disaster recovery-as-a-service (DRaaS) platform. It provides automatic replication, failover, and recovery of workloads hosted in Azure or on-premises.

Features:

- Continuous replication for low RPO
- Application-consistent snapshots
- Custom recovery plans for orchestrated failover
- Support for Azure-to-Azure, on-prem-to-Azure, and Hyper-V/VMware

Supported Scenarios:

- Azure VMs across regions
- On-premises to Azure VM failover
- Hybrid apps with SQL Server, SharePoint, etc.

Enable replication for an Azure VM

```
az backup vault create --name myVault --resource-group myResourceGroup --location eastus
az site-recovery protection-container create --vault-name myVault --fabric-name Azure \
  --name myProtectionContainer
```

ASR simplifies complex failover scenarios, especially when combined with **Recovery Plans** that script the order of service restarts and handle dependencies.

Region-Based Disaster Recovery Strategies

Active-Active (Hot-Hot)

All regions are live and serve traffic concurrently. Ensures the best RTO and RPO but is the most expensive.

- Use Azure Front Door or Traffic Manager for routing

- Requires data replication and conflict resolution (e.g., Cosmos DB multi-master)

- Good for global SaaS applications

Active-Passive (Hot-Cold)

One region serves traffic; another remains on standby.

- Use Traffic Manager with **priority** **routing**

- Replicate databases using geo-replication or failover groups

- Lower cost than active-active, with slightly higher RTO

Warm Standby

The secondary region is running at reduced capacity and scaled up during failover.

- Faster than cold but more cost-effective than hot-hot

- Common for e-commerce and mid-criticality business apps

Cold Standby

Resources in the secondary region are stopped or not provisioned until disaster strikes.

- Longest RTO, lowest cost

- Suitable for archival or regulatory systems with infrequent access

---

Data Replication in DR Scenarios

Azure offers multiple replication options depending on the service and recovery requirements:

Data Service	Replication Option	DR Usage
Azure Blob Storage	GRS / RA-GRS / GZRS	Cross-region data recovery
Azure SQL Database	Active geo-replication / Auto-failover group	Active-passive deployments
Cosmos DB	Multi-region writes	Global write/read failover
Azure Files	GRS (preview for Premium tier)	Secondary region accessibility
Virtual Machines	Azure Site Recovery	Full VM failover and recovery

---

Application and Infrastructure Recovery

To support full-stack recovery:

- Use **Azure Resource Manager (ARM)** or **Bicep** templates to re-deploy infrastructure
- Store templates and parameters in a version-controlled repository
- Use **Terraform** for multi-cloud or custom orchestration
- Export NSGs, route tables, DNS zones for rehydration

```
# Deploy infrastructure from Bicep
az deployment group create \
  --resource-group DRRegionRG \
  --template-file infrastructure.bicep \
  --parameters @dr-params.json
```

This Infrastructure-as-Code (IaC) approach allows fast, repeatable environment recreation.

Automating Disaster Recovery Workflows

Azure provides several tools to automate DR operations:

- **Recovery Plans** in ASR for sequenced failover
- **Azure Automation** for failover scripts and runbooks
- **Logic Apps** to orchestrate alerts and actions across services
- **GitHub Actions / Azure DevOps** pipelines for DR drills and testing

These automations reduce RTO by eliminating manual intervention during high-stress situations.

Security and Compliance in DR

Disaster recovery processes must be secure and auditable:

- Use **Role-Based Access Control (RBAC)** to restrict failover actions
- Store recovery credentials and keys in **Azure Key Vault**
- Enable **Activity Log Alerts** for DR actions
- Maintain a **DR runbook and audit log**

Ensure DR plans meet **industry-specific standards** (ISO, HIPAA, GDPR) with regular assessments and penetration testing.

Testing and Validation

A DR plan is only effective if it's regularly tested. Testing validates not only the technical feasibility but also operational readiness.

Types of DR Tests:

- **Planned failover**: Controlled environment to validate replication and failback.

- **Unplanned failover simulation**: Tests reaction to real-world disruptions.

- **Tabletop exercises**: Non-technical runthrough of roles and communications.

- **Chaos engineering**: Intentionally disrupt components to evaluate resilience.

Metrics to Track:

- Time to detect failure

- Time to initiate failover

- Recovery time (RTO)

- Data loss window (RPO)

- Communication effectiveness

Use **Azure Monitor**, **Application Insights**, and **Log Analytics** to analyze DR drill performance and identify improvement areas.

Cost Optimization for DR

DR planning should balance availability with cost:

- Use **automation to scale down** warm standby environments until needed

- Select **LRS storage** for backups if cross-region isn't required

- Use **serverless** or **consumption-based** resources in standby regions

- Apply **tags and budgets** to track DR resource spending

Real-World Disaster Recovery Architecture

Case: Financial Services Application

- Region: East US (primary), Central US (secondary)

- Architecture:

107 | Scale Smart

- Front Door for global traffic management
- Azure App Service (active-active)
- Cosmos DB with multi-region writes
- Azure Key Vault replicated manually
- Azure DNS with failover scripts
- Testing: Bi-annual failover drills, monthly configuration syncs

---

Conclusion

Disaster recovery in Azure is not a one-size-fits-all solution. It requires a strategic blend of regional architecture, service-specific replication, automated failover orchestration, and continuous testing. With services like Azure Site Recovery, geo-redundant storage, automated infrastructure provisioning, and distributed data platforms, Azure provides all the tools needed to meet diverse business continuity goals.

A well-planned DR strategy is your insurance policy against the unexpected—one that minimizes downtime, preserves data integrity, protects reputation, and ensures regulatory compliance. When disaster strikes, being prepared isn't optional—it's essential.

Chapter 5: Security and Governance in Azure Architectures

Identity and Access Management with Azure AD

Identity is the new perimeter in cloud computing. As organizations move away from traditional, perimeter-based security models to a **zero trust** approach, managing identities and controlling access becomes the foundation of secure architecture in Azure. **Azure Active Directory (Azure AD)** is Microsoft's identity and access management (IAM) solution, enabling secure authentication, authorization, and identity governance for users, applications, and services across hybrid and cloud environments.

This section delves into how Azure AD supports modern IAM strategies, its integration across Azure services, key capabilities, implementation best practices, and architectural patterns for secure, scalable identity management.

Understanding Azure Active Directory

Azure AD is a **cloud-based identity platform** that provides:

- **Authentication** (who you are)
- **Authorization** (what you can access)
- **Identity** lifecycle **management**
- **Federation** and **single** **sign-on** **(SSO)**
- **Multi-factor** **authentication** **(MFA)**
- **Conditional** **access** **policies**
- **B2B** and **B2C** **identity** **services**

Azure AD supports users, groups, applications, devices, and service principals, forming the basis of a secure, policy-driven identity architecture.

Core Concepts and Terminology

Term	Description

Tenant	A dedicated instance of Azure AD representing an organization
Object ID	A unique identifier for each identity object
User Principal Name	The login name of a user (e.g., john@contoso.com)
Service Principal	Identity used by applications or services to access Azure resources
Managed Identity	Automatically managed service identity for apps and services
Role Assignment	Binds a user, group, or principal to a role for resource access
Conditional Access	Policy engine for granting or blocking access based on context

Authentication in Azure AD

Azure AD supports multiple authentication protocols:

- **OpenID Connect (OIDC)** and **OAuth 2.0** for modern apps

- **SAML 2.0** for legacy enterprise integrations

- **WS-Federation** for older Microsoft applications

Use **Azure AD Connect** to synchronize on-premises Active Directory identities with Azure AD, enabling **hybrid identity** and **SSO** across cloud and on-prem environments.

```
# View currently signed-in user
az ad signed-in-user show
```

Authorization with Role-Based Access Control (RBAC)

RBAC is Azure's native authorization model that controls access to resources at the **subscription**, **resource group**, or **resource** level.

RBAC Roles:

- **Built-in roles**: Owner, Contributor, Reader, etc.

- **Custom roles**: Define precise permissions using JSON

- **Scope**: Assign roles at multiple levels for inheritance

```
# Assign Reader role to a user at resource group level
az role assignment create \
  --assignee user@domain.com \
  --role Reader \
  --resource-group myResourceGroup
```

RBAC is **stateless** and evaluates access on each request based on assignments. Use **least privilege** principles—grant only the minimum permissions required.

Managed Identities for Azure Resources

Managed Identities eliminate the need to manage credentials in your code. Azure handles the lifecycle of these identities, and they can be assigned to:

- Virtual Machines
- App Services
- Azure Functions
- Azure Kubernetes Service
- Logic Apps

There are two types:

1. **System-assigned**: Tied to the lifecycle of a resource
2. **User-assigned**: Standalone identity that can be shared across resources

```
# Assign a system-managed identity to a VM
az vm identity assign --name myVM --resource-group myRG
```

Use Managed Identities to authenticate securely to:

- Azure Key Vault
- Azure SQL Database

- Storage   accounts

- REST   APIs   secured   with   Azure   AD

Conditional Access Policies

Conditional Access is a powerful tool to enforce context-aware access controls. Policies can be based on:

- User/group

- Location

- Device   compliance

- Risk   level

- Application   sensitivity

Common Use Cases:

- Require   MFA   for   users   outside   the   corporate   network

- Block   legacy   authentication   protocols

- Restrict   access   to   high-privilege   apps   from   unmanaged   devices

```
# Sample Conditional Access policy logic
if (user in HR group) and (location == unknown) then
    require MFA
```

Monitor policy effectiveness through **Sign-In Logs** and **Azure Monitor**.

Multi-Factor Authentication (MFA)

MFA adds an extra layer of security by requiring two or more of:

- Something   you   know   (password)

- Something   you   have   (device,   app)

- Something you are (biometrics)

Azure MFA supports:

- Authenticator app
- SMS/phone call
- Hardware tokens (FIDO2, OATH)
- Biometric integration with Windows Hello

MFA can be enforced via:

- Conditional Access
- Security Defaults
- Per-user configuration

Enable **MFA for all administrative accounts** and critical applications as a baseline security control.

Identity Protection and Risk Management

Azure AD includes **Identity Protection**, which uses machine learning to detect suspicious sign-ins and compromised accounts.

It classifies risks as:

- **Low**: Unfamiliar sign-in properties
- **Medium**: Sign-ins from anonymizing IPs (Tor, VPN)
- **High**: Known leaked credentials

Responses include:

- Blocking access
- Requiring password reset

- Triggering   MFA

Enable reporting and alerts to respond proactively to threats.

Azure AD B2B and B2C

Azure AD B2B

- Enables   secure   collaboration   with   external   partners

- Uses   guest   accounts   in   your   directory

- Enforces   your   organization's   Conditional   Access   and   MFA   policies

```
# Invite B2B user
az ad user create --display-name "Guest User" --user-principal-name guest@external.com --
password MyPassword!
```

Azure AD B2C

- Identity   management   for   consumer-facing   apps

- Customizable   sign-up,   sign-in,   and   profile   management

- Supports   external   IDPs   (Google,   Facebook,   etc.)

B2C is ideal for building branded, scalable authentication flows in multi-tenant SaaS and public platforms.

Monitoring and Auditing

Azure provides robust tools for monitoring identity-related activity:

- **Azure AD Sign-In Logs**: View sign-in attempts, status, location, app

- **Audit Logs**: Track changes to users, roles, and policies

- **Microsoft Sentinel**: SIEM integration for deep analysis

- **Log Analytics**: Custom queries and dashboards

Use queries like:

```
SigninLogs
| where ResultType != 0
| summarize count() by UserPrincipalName, AppDisplayName
```

Enable **diagnostic settings** to forward logs to storage, Event Hub, or SIEM platforms.

Governance with Identity Lifecycle Management

Manage the entire lifecycle of digital identities using:

- **Access Reviews**: Periodic validation of group and role assignments

- **Privileged Identity Management (PIM)**: Just-in-time elevation of roles

- **Entitlement Management**: Automate resource access packages

- **Self-service group management**: Empower users under policy control

PIM is especially valuable for high-privilege accounts—ensuring that elevated permissions are **temporary, approved, and auditable**.

Best Practices for Identity and Access Management

1. **Implement least privilege access** via RBAC and custom roles.

2. **Enforce MFA** for all users, especially admins.

3. **Use Conditional Access** to adapt to risk and context.

4. **Leverage Managed Identities** to eliminate hardcoded secrets.

5. **Regularly review access and assignments** using Access Reviews.

6. **Monitor sign-in behavior** and suspicious activity using Identity Protection.

7. **Isolate administrative roles** using PIM and separate accounts.

8. **Integrate IAM into CI/CD pipelines** to enforce policies early.

9. **Use B2B and B2C appropriately** for external identities.

10. **Back up policies and configurations** using ARM templates or Terraform.

Conclusion

In Azure, identity is the control plane of the cloud. Azure Active Directory provides a comprehensive platform for managing users, applications, and access securely and at scale. By implementing strong identity controls—such as RBAC, Conditional Access, MFA, and identity governance—architects can build environments that are both user-friendly and secure.

Identity and access management isn't just about securing logins. It's about defining how people, apps, and services interact within your digital estate. Azure AD makes this interaction secure, observable, and governable—forming the backbone of any resilient, compliant cloud architecture.

Network Security Groups and Firewalls

Securing network traffic is fundamental to safeguarding resources and applications in the cloud. In Azure, this is accomplished through a layered approach that includes **Network Security Groups (NSGs)** and **firewall solutions**. These tools form the first line of defense, controlling inbound and outbound traffic, isolating workloads, and protecting against malicious attacks, both internal and external.

This section provides an in-depth exploration of Azure's core network security controls, explains their design and implementation, and discusses best practices to architect a secure and scalable network environment.

Understanding Network Security Groups (NSGs)

Network Security Groups (NSGs) are Azure's built-in tool to control network traffic to and from Azure resources. NSGs contain **security rules** that allow or deny traffic based on:

- Source and destination IP

- Source and destination port

- Protocol (TCP/UDP)

- Direction (inbound/outbound)

NSGs can be applied at two levels:

1. **Subnet-level**: Applies to all resources within a subnet

2. **NIC-level**: Applies to an individual virtual machine's network interface

NSG rules are **stateful**, meaning return traffic is automatically allowed for an approved outbound request.

NSG Rule Example:

Priority	Name	Direction	Protocol	Port	Source	Action
100	AllowHTTP	Inbound	TCP	80	Any	Allow
200	AllowSSH	Inbound	TCP	22	203.0.113.5	Allow
3000	DenyAllInbound	Inbound	*	*	Any	Deny

```
# Create a basic NSG
az network nsg create \
  --resource-group myResourceGroup \
  --name myNSG

# Add a rule to allow inbound SSH
az network nsg rule create \
  --nsg-name myNSG \
  --resource-group myResourceGroup \
  --name AllowSSH \
  --priority 100 \
  --direction Inbound \
  --access Allow \
  --protocol Tcp \
  --destination-port-ranges 22 \
  --source-address-prefixes 203.0.113.5
```

NSG Design Considerations

- **Use subnet-level NSGs for shared services** (e.g., App Gateway subnet).

- **Use NIC-level NSGs for application-specific policies** (e.g., isolate VMs in same subnet).

- **Keep default deny rule at lowest priority** to block unapproved traffic.

- **Use service tags** (e.g., Internet, VirtualNetwork, AzureLoadBalancer) for easier rule management.

- **Use application security groups (ASGs)** to group similar workloads dynamically and apply NSG rules to groups rather than IPs.

```
# Example of using service tag
az network nsg rule create \
  --nsg-name myNSG \
  --resource-group myResourceGroup \
  --name AllowLoadBalancer \
  --priority 200 \
  --direction Inbound \
  --access Allow \
  --protocol Tcp \
  --source-address-prefix AzureLoadBalancer \
  --destination-port-range 80
```

Application Security Groups (ASGs)

ASGs simplify large-scale deployments by logically grouping VMs and applying NSG rules at the group level instead of managing individual IP addresses.

Use cases include:

- Isolating application tiers (web, app, database)

- Creating zone-based security models (frontend, backend)

- Managing dynamic infrastructure at scale

```
# Create an ASG
az network asg create \
  --resource-group myResourceGroup \
  --name WebServers

# Associate VM NIC with ASG
az network nic update \
  --name myNic \
  --resource-group myResourceGroup \
  --application-security-groups WebServers
```

ASGs are ideal for **microsegmentation**, a principle of zero trust architecture.

Azure Firewall: Advanced Network Security

While NSGs are sufficient for many scenarios, **Azure Firewall** provides **stateful, fully managed, centralized network protection** for all traffic flows in and out of a virtual network.

Features:

- Fully stateful inspection

- Application rules for FQDN-based filtering

- Network rules for IP/port/protocol control

- Threat intelligence-based filtering (alert or deny)

- Integration with Azure Monitor and third-party SIEMs

- Forced tunneling to redirect internet traffic through central inspection

```
# Create Azure Firewall
az network firewall create \
  --name myFirewall \
  --resource-group myResourceGroup \
  --location eastus

# Add a network rule collection
az network firewall network-rule collection rule add \
  --firewall-name myFirewall \
  --collection-name AllowWeb \
  --name AllowHTTP \
  --rule-type NetworkRule \
  --action Allow \
  --priority 100 \
  --protocols TCP \
  --source-addresses '*' \
  --destination-addresses '*' \
  --destination-ports 80
```

Azure Firewall supports **multiple public IPs**, **SNAT**, and **IP Groups** for efficient traffic control.

Azure Firewall vs. NSG

Feature	NSG	Azure Firewall
Rule Type	IP/Port/Protocol	Application and network rules
Stateful	Yes	Yes
Logging	Basic via NSG flow logs	Full logging via Azure Monitor
Threat Intelligence	No	Yes (block known malicious IPs)
Centralized Deployment	No (per subnet/NIC)	Yes (hub-spoke model)
FQDN Filtering	No	Yes
TLS Inspection	No	Yes (preview)

Use **NSGs** for **basic traffic filtering** and **Azure Firewall** for **advanced inspection and control** in enterprise-grade scenarios.

Azure Web Application Firewall (WAF)

When protecting HTTP/S workloads, use **Azure Application Gateway with WAF** or **Azure Front Door with WAF** to inspect web traffic at Layer 7.

Capabilities:

- OWASP Core Rule Set (CRS) protection
- Custom rules and rate limiting
- Bot protection (preview)
- Logging, alerts, and diagnostics
- IP restriction and geo-filtering

```
# Enable WAF on Application Gateway
az network application-gateway waf-config set \
  --enabled true \
  --gateway-name myAppGateway \
  --resource-group myResourceGroup \
```

```
--firewall-mode Prevention \
--rule-set-type OWASP \
--rule-set-version 3.2
```

WAFs are essential for defending against SQL injection, XSS, and other web-layer threats.

Logging and Monitoring Network Security

Monitor NSG and firewall activity using:

- **NSG Flow Logs**: Track inbound/outbound traffic flows at the NIC level

- **Traffic Analytics**: Visualize NSG traffic trends and hotspots

- **Azure Firewall Logs**: Log all rule matches, denied traffic, and threats

- **Azure Monitor + Log Analytics**: Query, visualize, and alert on network events

```
AzureDiagnostics
| where ResourceType == "AZUREFIREWALLS"
| where Category == "AzureFirewallNetworkRule"
| summarize count() by msg_s
```

Export logs to **Log Analytics**, **Storage**, or **Event Hubs** for compliance and retention.

Best Practices for Securing Azure Networks

1. **Deny by default**: Allow only explicitly required traffic.

2. **Use NSGs at both subnet and NIC level** for layered control.

3. **Group workloads logically with ASGs** to simplify rule management.

4. **Use Azure Firewall in hub-spoke networks** for centralized security.

5. **Deploy WAF for web workloads** to prevent application-layer attacks.

6. **Limit management port access (SSH, RDP)** with IP whitelisting or Just-in-Time access.

7. **Monitor and alert on traffic anomalies** using Azure Sentinel or Log Analytics.

8. **Review NSG rules regularly** to eliminate unused or over-permissive access.

9. **Segment networks** by environment (dev/test/prod) using separate VNets or subnets.

10. **Integrate with Azure Policy** to enforce rule standards across environments.

Conclusion

Network Security Groups and Azure Firewall together form a powerful and flexible framework for securing Azure environments. NSGs offer lightweight, rule-based filtering ideal for microsegmentation and tiered security, while Azure Firewall delivers deep packet inspection, centralized control, and enterprise-scale protections.

By combining NSGs, ASGs, firewalls, and web application firewalls—alongside continuous monitoring and policy enforcement—organizations can build resilient and secure network architectures that scale with their applications and adapt to evolving threat landscapes. In a world where cyber threats are persistent and evolving, proactive and layered network security is not optional—it's essential.

Azure Policy and Role-Based Access Control (RBAC)

Governance in Azure ensures that cloud resources are deployed, configured, and used in compliance with your organization's security, operational, and business rules. Two key services enable this: **Azure Policy**, which enforces compliance through rule-based governance, and **Role-Based Access Control (RBAC)**, which governs who can perform what actions on which resources. Together, they form the cornerstone of secure and compliant Azure resource management.

This section explores both services in detail, including their components, implementation strategies, and best practices for building secure, controlled, and scalable environments.

What Is Azure Policy?

Azure Policy is a service in Azure that allows you to create, assign, and manage policy definitions that enforce rules and effects on resources. These policies help ensure that all deployed resources meet your organization's standards and compliance requirements.

Key Capabilities:

- **Enforce tagging rules** (e.g., require cost center tags)

- **Restrict   locations   for   resources**

- Control allowed VM SKUs or disk types
- Require encryption for storage accounts
- Audit insecure configurations
- Deploy remediation actions (DeployIfNotExists)

Azure Policy can **deny**, **audit**, **modify**, **append**, or **deploy** resources depending on policy logic.

Azure Policy Structure

A policy definition includes:

- **Display Name** and **Description**
- **Policy Rule** (conditions and effect)
- **Parameters** (for reusability)

Example: Restricting VM locations

```
{
 "if": {
  "not": {
   "field": "location",
   "in": ["eastus", "westeurope"]
  }
 },
 "then": {
  "effect": "deny"
 }
}
```

Policies can be grouped into **Initiatives**—collections of policy definitions—applied together to enforce broader compliance objectives (e.g., PCI-DSS, ISO 27001).

Assigning and Scoping Policies

Azure Policy can be assigned at multiple scopes:

- **Management**   **Group**

- **Subscription**

- **Resource**   **Group**

- **Individual**   **Resource**

```
# Assign a built-in policy to enforce tag
az policy assignment create \
  --name requireCostCenterTag \
  --policy "Require a tag and its value" \
  --params '{ "tagName": { "value": "costCenter" } }' \
  --scope "/subscriptions/xxxxxxxx-xxxx-xxxx-xxxx-xxxxxxxxxxxx"
```

Use **management groups** to enforce organizational-wide policies at scale. Assigning policies at higher scopes ensures **inheritance** and consistency.

Policy Effects

Azure Policy supports multiple effects that determine the action taken when conditions are met:

Effect	Description
Deny	Prevents non-compliant resources from being deployed
Audit	Flags non-compliant resources but does not block them
Append	Adds specified properties during deployment
Modify	Alters resource properties to make them compliant
DeployIfNotExists	Triggers automatic deployment of required resources (e.g., diagnostics)

Use Audit mode for early policy rollouts, and transition to Deny as confidence grows.

Policy Compliance and Remediation

Azure Policy tracks compliance state in the **Compliance Blade**. It shows:

- Total   resources   evaluated

- Non-compliant   resources

- Historical   compliance   trend

- Per-policy   breakdown

For supported effects, you can trigger **remediation tasks** to bring existing resources into compliance.

```
# Start remediation task
az policy remediation create \
 --name remediateDiagnosticSettings \
 --policy-assignment requireDiagnosticSettings \
 --resource-group myResourceGroup
```

Role-Based Access Control (RBAC)

Azure RBAC enables fine-grained access management by assigning permissions to users, groups, or service principals for specific resources.

Core Concepts:

- **Role Definition**: A collection of permissions (actions)

- **Role Assignment**: Binding of a principal to a role at a scope

- **Scope**: The boundary of the role's effect (management group, subscription, resource group,   or   resource)

Azure includes **built-in roles** (e.g., Owner, Contributor, Reader) and supports **custom roles**.

```
# Assign Contributor role to a user for a resource group
az role assignment create \
 --assignee user@domain.com \
 --role Contributor \
 --resource-group myResourceGroup
```

Built-in RBAC Roles

Role	Description
Owner	Full access, including access management
Contributor	Full access, except managing access
Reader	View only access
User Access Admin	Can manage access permissions
Storage Blob Data Reader	Read-only access to Blob containers and blobs

Custom Roles

Custom roles allow you to define precise permissions tailored to your organizational needs.

```
{
 "Name": "CustomTagEditor",
 "IsCustom": true,
 "Description": "Can update resource tags",
 "Actions": [
  "Microsoft.Resources/tags/write",
  "Microsoft.Resources/subscriptions/resourceGroups/read"
 ],
 "AssignableScopes": [
  "/subscriptions/xxxxxxxx-xxxx-xxxx-xxxx-xxxxxxxxxxxx"
 ]
}
```

RBAC vs Azure Policy

Feature	Azure Policy	Azure RBAC
Purpose	Enforce configuration/compliance	Control access/permissions
Enforcement	Deny, audit, modify, auto-deploy	Allow based on assigned permissions
Target	Resource state	Resource actions

Scoping	MG, subscription, RG, resource	MG, subscription, RG, resource
Ideal for	Governance, compliance, remediation	Least privilege access control

Together, they provide **complementary** controls—RBAC governs *who* can do *what*, while Policy governs *what* is allowed.

Best Practices for Policy and RBAC

1. **Use management groups** to assign org-wide policies and access controls.

2. **Audit before deny**—roll out policies in audit mode to measure impact.

3. **Follow least privilege**—only grant access required for a role.

4. **Use custom roles** where built-in roles don't meet your needs.

5. **Assign permissions at the lowest practical scope**.

6. **Document access assignments** and policy rationales for audits.

7. **Use initiatives** to group related policies (e.g., CIS, NIST, PCI).

8. **Remediate non-compliant resources regularly**.

9. **Log all role changes** with Azure Activity Logs.

10. **Use Azure Policy to enforce tagging** for cost and environment classification.

Monitoring Governance

Governance tools generate rich telemetry:

- **Azure Activity Logs**: Tracks RBAC role assignments and policy changes

- **Azure Monitor + Log Analytics**: Analyzes policy compliance over time

- **Compliance Blade**: Dashboards for each policy assignment

- **Azure Advisor**: Identifies over-privileged access and recommends changes

- **Azure Purview (now Microsoft Purview)**: Catalogs data and classifies sensitive information in compliance contexts

---

Real-World Scenario

Case: Multinational Enterprise

- Use **management groups** for global, regional, and department-level control

- Apply **RBAC at subscription level** for platform teams, and **resource group level** for app teams

- Assign **initiative with 30+ policies** to enforce tagging, location, and diagnostic settings

- Use **Azure Blueprints** to package governance into templates for new subscriptions

---

Conclusion

Azure Policy and Role-Based Access Control are foundational to enforcing security, compliance, and operational discipline in Azure. Policies ensure that resources conform to governance standards, while RBAC controls access at every level of your environment. Used together, they support a robust governance model that empowers agility without sacrificing control.

A secure Azure architecture isn't just about locking down services—it's about enabling innovation within a framework of transparency, accountability, and enforceable policy. By mastering Azure Policy and RBAC, cloud architects can deliver systems that are not only secure and compliant but also structured for growth and collaboration.

Compliance Frameworks and Best Practices

Cloud adoption brings immense scalability, agility, and innovation opportunities—but it also comes with a mandate to protect data, ensure privacy, and maintain regulatory compliance. In Microsoft Azure, compliance isn't an afterthought—it's deeply integrated into the platform. Azure offers a robust set of tools, certifications, and frameworks that enable organizations to build and maintain compliant architectures across regulated industries including healthcare, finance, education, and government.

This section explores the key compliance frameworks supported by Azure, outlines governance best practices, and provides architectural patterns and tools to meet compliance mandates efficiently and securely.

The Role of Compliance in Cloud Architecture

Compliance ensures that cloud systems align with legal, regulatory, and organizational policies. This includes:

- **Data privacy laws** (e.g., GDPR, CCPA)

- **Industry-specific regulations** (e.g., HIPAA, PCI-DSS, FedRAMP)

- **Security best practices** (e.g., ISO 27001, CIS benchmarks)

- **Operational guidelines** (e.g., NIST, SOC)

In Azure, compliance is achieved through a combination of:

- Built-in platform controls

- Governance policies

- Secure service configuration

- Continuous monitoring and auditing

Microsoft Azure Compliance Offerings

Azure is certified across a wide range of international and industry-specific compliance standards:

Framework	Description
ISO 27001	Global standard for information security management systems
SOC 1, 2, 3	Controls related to financial reporting and data processing
GDPR	European Union data privacy regulation
HIPAA/HITECH	US healthcare data protection laws
PCI-DSS	Payment Card Industry Data Security Standard

FedRAMP High US federal government security accreditation

CIS Benchmarks Best practices for secure configuration of systems and services

NIST 800-53 US security and privacy controls for federal information systems

Microsoft provides detailed documentation and audit reports in the **Microsoft Trust Center** and **Service Trust Portal**.

Azure Compliance Tools

Microsoft Purview Compliance Manager

A centralized compliance dashboard that:

- Assesses compliance with over 300 regulations and standards

- Provides control mapping for Microsoft services

- Offers actionable improvement recommendations

- Tracks compliance score over time

```
# Enable regulatory compliance assessments via Azure Policy
az policy assignment create \
  --name EnableHIPAA \
  --scope "/subscriptions/xxxx-xxxx" \
  --policy-set-definition "HIPAA-HITRUST"
```

Azure Blueprints

Blueprints allow organizations to define a repeatable set of Azure resources and governance policies that comply with a given standard.

Example: Deploy a **PCI-DSS Blueprint** that includes:

- Predefined policies (e.g., audit VMs without endpoint protection)

- Role assignments

- Resource locks

- ARM templates for required resources

Azure Policy Regulatory Compliance

Policy initiatives can be mapped to specific compliance domains, like:

- Identity and access control
- Encryption
- Monitoring and logging
- Backup and recovery

Use the **Regulatory Compliance Dashboard** to monitor posture against frameworks such as **CIS**, **NIST**, **PCI-DSS**, and **UK NHS**.

Encryption and Data Protection

To meet most compliance mandates, data must be encrypted:

- **At rest** using Azure Storage Service Encryption, SQL TDE, and Azure Disk Encryption
- **In transit** using HTTPS/TLS 1.2 or higher
- **In use** using confidential computing (e.g., Intel SGX)

Azure supports **Customer Managed Keys (CMK)** via Azure Key Vault to ensure control over encryption processes.

```
# Assign a CMK to an Azure Storage Account
az storage account encryption-scope create \
  --name myScope \
  --account-name mystorageaccount \
  --resource-group myRG \
  --key-uri https://mykeyvault.vault.azure.net/keys/mykey
```

Use **Azure Defender for Cloud** to monitor encryption settings and receive alerts when non-compliant configurations are detected.

Identity and Access Controls

A core requirement in virtually all compliance frameworks is enforcing strong access controls:

- **Use Azure Active Directory for centralized identity management**

- **Enable Multi-Factor Authentication (MFA)** for all users, especially administrators

- **Use Conditional Access** to enforce contextual policies

- **Limit privileged access with Azure AD Privileged Identity Management (PIM)**

All access changes and login attempts should be logged via **Azure Monitor**, **Sign-In Logs**, and **Activity Logs**, and forwarded to **Microsoft Sentinel** for SIEM capabilities.

Network Security Compliance

To meet compliance objectives for segmentation, traffic control, and isolation:

- Implement **Network Security Groups (NSGs)** and **Azure Firewall** for micro-segmentation

- Use **Private Endpoints** for secure, private access to services

- Deploy **Web Application Firewall (WAF)** to protect HTTP/S workloads

- Enable **DDoS Protection Standard** for production environments

Use **Azure Policy** to enforce security configuration standards such as:

```
{
  "if": {
    "not": {
      "field": "Microsoft.Network/networkSecurityGroups/securityRules[*].access",
      "equals": "Deny"
    }
  },
  "then": {
    "effect": "audit"
  }
}
```

Monitoring and Auditing

Continuous monitoring is required to maintain compliance and detect violations.

Azure offers:

- **Azure Monitor** for metrics and logs

- **Log Analytics Workspace** for querying across services

- **Microsoft Sentinel** for SIEM and SOAR capabilities

- **Diagnostic settings** to send logs to storage, Event Hubs, or Log Analytics

- **Activity Logs and Resource Logs** to track changes and access patterns

Use **Change Tracking**, **Update Management**, and **Inventory Solutions** in **Azure Automation** to monitor drift from compliant baselines.

Compliance Automation and CI/CD Integration

Embed compliance checks in your CI/CD pipeline to enforce security and regulatory checks before deployment.

Use tools like:

- **Terraform + Sentinel/OPA**: Prevent non-compliant infrastructure-as-code

- **Azure DevOps Gates**: Evaluate Azure Policy and scan results during release

- **Pre-deployment hooks**: Enforce tagging, encryption, or access policies

```
# Sample Azure DevOps YAML with policy gate
- task: AzureCLI@2
  inputs:
    scriptType: 'bash'
    scriptLocation: 'inlineScript'
    inlineScript: |
      az policy state list --query "[?complianceState=='NonCompliant']"
```

Automation is key to achieving and maintaining compliance at scale in agile environments.

Documentation and Evidence Gathering

For internal audits or external assessments, ensure:

- Policies and procedures are documented
- Role assignments and access reviews are recorded
- Evidence (screenshots, logs, settings) is collected and stored securely
- Data protection impact assessments (DPIAs) are performed for sensitive workloads

Use tools like **Microsoft Compliance Manager** to export reports, generate evidence, and provide proof of control implementation.

Best Practices for Maintaining Compliance

1. **Use management groups** to enforce global policies and blueprints.
2. **Enable audit trails** and ensure they are immutable and retained.
3. **Limit access with RBAC and PIM,** and review regularly.
4. **Encrypt all sensitive data at rest and in transit** with CMK where required.
5. **Use only compliant services and deployment regions** as per your industry.
6. **Automate remediation and drift detection** via Azure Policy.
7. **Conduct regular DR drills and backup audits** to validate recoverability.
8. **Use regulatory compliance initiatives** from Azure Policy or Blueprints.
9. **Integrate compliance checks in CI/CD pipelines**.
10. **Train developers and engineers** on the compliance implications of their roles.

Conclusion

In today's digital ecosystem, compliance is not optional—it's an ongoing, strategic imperative. Azure provides a comprehensive suite of tools, certifications, and best practices to help you achieve and maintain compliance in a constantly evolving regulatory landscape. From data protection and identity control to audit logging and infrastructure governance, compliance is deeply woven into the Azure platform.

By aligning your architecture with relevant frameworks, enforcing automated policies, and maintaining continuous visibility into your cloud environment, you can protect sensitive data, reduce risk, and build customer trust—while enabling your organization to move quickly, securely, and confidently in the cloud.

Chapter 6: Cost Optimization Strategies

Azure Pricing Models and Calculators

Effective cost management is one of the most crucial aspects of designing and operating cloud-based solutions. In Microsoft Azure, resources are priced based on a variety of factors including service type, usage metrics, data egress, reserved commitments, and licensing models. Understanding Azure's pricing structure and leveraging available tools like the **Azure Pricing Calculator** and **Total Cost of Ownership (TCO) Calculator** enables organizations to forecast, control, and reduce their cloud spending effectively.

This section explores the core Azure pricing models, key pricing considerations for different services, how to use Azure's cost estimation tools, and best practices to integrate cost awareness into your architecture and operational processes.

Understanding Azure Pricing Models

Azure provides several pricing models that cater to different workloads and budget strategies:

1. Pay-As-You-Go (PAYG)

- **Billing**: Per second/minute/hour depending on resource type
- **Flexibility**: No upfront commitment; start and stop resources at will
- **Use Cases**: Dev/test environments, dynamic or unpredictable workloads

2. Reserved Instances (RI)

- **Billing**: One- or three-year upfront or monthly commitment
- **Discounts**: Up to 72% off PAYG prices
- **Use Cases**: Predictable workloads, production systems

```
# View available reservation SKUs for a region
az consumption reservation catalog show --subscription <sub-id> --region eastus
```

3. Spot Pricing

- **Billing**: Based on unused Azure capacity

- **Discounts**: Up to 90% off standard prices
- **Volatility**: Resources can be evicted at any time
- **Use Cases**: Batch jobs, stateless, fault-tolerant applications

4. Hybrid Benefit

- **Eligibility**: Bring your on-prem Windows Server or SQL Server licenses
- **Benefit**: Use existing licenses to save up to 85% on VMs and SQL DBs
- **Use Cases**: Enterprises with Software Assurance or existing licenses

---

Key Cost Components

Azure resource costs vary by region and resource configuration. The primary cost categories include:

- **Compute**: VM size, uptime, OS type, scaling configuration
- **Storage**: Data stored, redundancy tier, transaction volume
- **Networking**: Data transfer between regions, public IP usage, VPN gateways
- **Databases**: Provisioned throughput, storage, backup retention
- **Licensing**: Software licenses included or brought separately (e.g., SQL, Windows)
- **Support Plans**: Developer, Standard, Professional Direct, Enterprise

Always refer to the Azure Pricing page for up-to-date information.

Azure Pricing Calculator

The **Azure Pricing Calculator** is a web-based tool that helps you estimate the cost of Azure services based on your expected usage.

Features:

- Add multiple services and configure details

- Adjust usage frequency, region, support plan
- Export estimates to Excel or shareable links
- Apply Azure Hybrid Benefit and reserved instance options
- View monthly and upfront cost breakdowns

Example Use Case:

Estimate the cost for:

- 3 VMs (Standard_D2s_v4)
- 1 App Service Plan (P1v2)
- 1 SQL Database (General Purpose, 100 DTUs)
- 1 Storage Account (RA-GRS, 1TB)

Steps:

1. Navigate to https://azure.com/pricing/calculator
2. Add services and configure parameters (e.g., region, instance size)
3. Enable discounts (e.g., 1-year RI, hybrid licensing)
4. View total estimated monthly cost

```
# Azure CLI does not support full pricing estimations but can assist in listing SKUs
az vm list-skus --location eastus --output table
```

Total Cost of Ownership (TCO) Calculator

The **TCO Calculator** helps enterprises estimate the long-term cost savings of migrating workloads from on-premises to Azure.

Inputs:

- Servers (CPU/RAM/storage)
- Databases

- Networking

- IT   labor   and   administration

- Software   licenses

Outputs:

- 3-year   comparison   of   on-prem   vs   Azure

- Capital   vs   operational   expenses

- Potential   savings   with   Hybrid   Benefits

This tool is especially helpful during the planning and budgeting phases of cloud migration.

Common Pricing Scenarios by Service

Virtual Machines

- Charged   per   second   (Linux)   or   per   minute   (Windows)

- Discounts   for   Reserved   Instances   and   Spot

- Additional   charges   for   disks,   public   IPs,   backup

Azure Functions

- Charged   based   on   execution   count   and   time   (GB-s)

- Free   tier: 1   million   executions/month

Azure App Services

- Shared,   Basic,   Standard,   Premium   tiers

- Charged   based   on   instance   count   and   size

Azure SQL Database

- DTU-based   or   vCore-based   pricing

- Elastic Pools help save on fluctuating multi-database workloads

Azure Blob Storage

- Charged by tier (Hot, Cool, Archive)
- Transaction costs increase as access frequency decreases
- Lifecycle rules help transition objects between tiers automatically

```
# Set storage tier using Azure CLI
az storage blob set-tier --account-name mystorageacct --container-name mycontainer --name
myblob --tier Cool
```

Cost-Aware Architecture Best Practices

1. **Right-size resources**: Choose VMs, DBs, and services appropriate to workload demand.

2. **Scale dynamically**: Use auto-scaling features to reduce idle resources.

3. **Use serverless where possible**: Pay only for what you use.

4. **Leverage reserved instances and Hybrid Benefit**: Apply when predictable workloads are present.

5. **Choose appropriate storage tiers**: Use Archive or Cool for infrequently accessed data.

6. **Consolidate workloads**: Use Elastic Pools, shared hosting, or containers.

7. **Monitor and alert**: Use Azure Cost Management and Budget Alerts.

8. **Apply tags for cost tracking**: Classify by project, department, or environment.

```
# Tag a resource for cost tracking
az tag create --resource-id
"/subscriptions/xxxxx/resourceGroups/myRG/providers/Microsoft.Compute/virtualMachines/
myVM" \
 --tags "Environment=Prod" "Project=ERP"
```

Azure Cost Management and Billing

Azure Cost Management + Billing is the core tool for analyzing and optimizing your Azure costs.

Capabilities:

- Budget creation and threshold alerts
- Cost analysis by resource, group, tag, or subscription
- Recommendations for underutilized resources
- Forecasting and trend analysis
- Custom dashboards and reports

Integrates with:

- Azure Advisor (cost-saving tips)
- Power BI (custom reports)
- APIs and automation scripts for enterprise cost governance

Licensing Optimization

Reduce cost further by managing licenses wisely:

- Use **Azure Hybrid Benefit** for Windows Server and SQL Server
- Consolidate licensing via **Microsoft Enterprise Agreements**
- Monitor third-party VM licenses via Azure Arc or BYOL (Bring Your Own License)

Real-World Example

Scenario: A SaaS company migrating from on-prem to Azure

- Migrated 50 Windows VMs using Reserved Instances (3-year)

- Applied Azure Hybrid Benefit
- Deployed SQL Managed Instance with reserved pricing
- Used Blob Archive tier for historical logs
- Monthly cost reduced from $72,000 (on-prem) to $34,000 (Azure)

Tools used:

- Azure Pricing Calculator
- Azure Migrate
- Azure Cost Management
- TCO Calculator

Conclusion

Cost optimization in Azure is not a one-time activity—it's an ongoing discipline integrated into architecture, development, and operations. By understanding the diverse pricing models, leveraging Azure's calculators and management tools, and adopting cloud-native best practices, you can significantly reduce your spend while improving agility and scalability.

Smart architecture is not just about performance and reliability—it's also about financial efficiency. In the next sections, we'll explore how monitoring usage and implementing budgeting strategies can further reduce operational overhead and improve your cloud ROI.

Monitoring and Analyzing Usage

Effectively managing cloud costs requires continuous visibility into resource consumption and usage trends. Microsoft Azure provides a comprehensive set of tools and services to **monitor, analyze, and optimize** resource usage. These capabilities help organizations identify inefficiencies, forecast future spending, detect anomalies, and implement data-driven cost control strategies.

This section explores the architecture of Azure usage monitoring, key tools for data analysis, automation strategies for real-time insights, and best practices for embedding cost awareness into your operational workflows.

Why Monitor Usage?

Monitoring usage is about more than just avoiding overspending—it's about accountability, transparency, and proactive management. Key goals include:

- **Preventing unexpected costs** through early detection

- **Identifying underutilized resources** for downsizing or termination

- **Tracking consumption per team/project/environment**

- **Forecasting growth trends** to inform budgeting

- **Supporting chargeback/showback** models in enterprise environments

By continuously analyzing usage data, you empower stakeholders with actionable intelligence to drive efficiency.

Azure Cost Management + Billing Overview

Azure provides an integrated platform for managing resource usage and cost called **Azure Cost Management + Billing**.

Core Features:

- Daily cost and usage data

- Budgeting and alerting

- Usage breakdown by service, region, resource group, or tag

- Forecasting and trend analysis

- Cost anomaly detection

- Recommendations (from Azure Advisor)

All data is available through:

- Azure Portal

- REST APIs

- Power BI connector

- SDKs and CLI

Accessing Usage Data

Azure Portal

Navigate to **Cost Management + Billing** → **Cost Analysis** to:

- View current and historical usage trends
- Group data by **subscription**, **service**, **location**, **tag**, or **resource**
- Apply filters (e.g., date range, resource type)
- Export to CSV or schedule reports

Azure CLI / REST API

You can extract usage and cost data programmatically using:

```
# List usage for the current billing period
az consumption usage list --start-date 2024-04-01 --end-date 2024-04-24 --output table
```

For detailed exports, use the **Usage Details API** or configure **Export to Storage**.

```
# Enable daily cost export to Storage
az costmanagement export create \
  --name dailyExport \
  --type Usage \
  --time-frame MonthToDate \
  --storage-account-id "/subscriptions/.../storageAccounts/myExportStorage" \
  --recurrence Daily
```

Azure Monitor Integration

Azure Monitor provides a telemetry platform for gathering metrics and logs across all Azure services. Key capabilities include:

- **Custom dashboards** for usage metrics (CPU, memory, requests)
- **Alerts** on unusual usage spikes
- **Integration with Log Analytics** for advanced querying

Use **Log Analytics Workspace** to query usage and cost telemetry.

```
UsageDetails
| summarize TotalCost=sum(Cost) by ResourceGroup, ResourceType
| order by TotalCost desc
```

You can also stream usage data into **Microsoft Sentinel** or **third-party SIEMs** for real-time alerting and compliance.

Tagging for Granular Visibility

Azure tags allow you to label resources with metadata such as:

- Environment (e.g., dev, test, prod)

- Department (e.g., finance, engineering)

- Project (e.g., ecommerce2025)

- Owner (e.g., jsmith@domain.com)

Tags are critical for usage segmentation and chargeback reporting.

```
# Apply tags to a VM
az tag update --resource-id
/subscriptions/xxx/resourceGroups/rg/providers/Microsoft.Compute/virtualMachines/vm01 \
--operation merge --tags Project=ecommerce2025 Owner=jsmith Environment=prod
```

Tagging best practices:

- Use standardized, enforceable tag names (enforced via Azure Policy)

- Tag all billable resources

- Periodically audit for missing or incorrect tags

Anomaly Detection and Alerts

Azure Cost Management automatically detects **cost anomalies**—sudden, unexplained increases in usage or spending.

To stay ahead:

- Enable **budget alerts** based on predefined thresholds

- Set up **usage alerts** per service, region, or tag

- Monitor unusual trends using **Azure Advisor cost recommendations**

```
# Create a budget with alert
az consumption budget create \
  --amount 500 \
  --category cost \
  --name MonthlyBudget \
  --resource-group myResourceGroup \
  --time-grain monthly \
  --start-date 2024-04-01 \
  --end-date 2024-12-31 \
  --notifications
actual_greater_than_80_percent="{'enabled':true,'operator':'GreaterThan','threshold':80,'contactEmails':['admin@contoso.com']}"
```

Forecasting and Trend Analysis

Azure Cost Management provides **forecasting tools** that project future usage based on current trends.

Key visualizations:

- Daily burn rate

- 30-day rolling average

- Forecast vs budget

For advanced needs, export usage data to **Power BI** for custom dashboards, trend analysis, and decision support.

Power BI usage data model includes:

- Cost and usage by tag

- Forecasting with predictive analytics

- Departmental cost allocation

- Budget   compliance

Chargeback and Showback Reporting

Larger enterprises use **chargeback** (internal billing) or **showback** (report-only) to assign cloud costs to business units or projects.

Steps:

1. Implement   consistent   tagging
2. Export   daily   usage   data
3. Group   costs   by   tag   values
4. Generate   dashboards   or   automated   reports

This model drives **accountability** and encourages **cost-conscious behavior** across teams.

Automating Cost Insights

Use Azure Automation, Logic Apps, or Azure Functions to:

- Auto-scale   or   shut   down   idle   resources
- Auto-tag   resources   based   on   naming   convention
- Generate   and   email   daily   usage   reports
- Sync   cost   data   with   internal   accounting   systems

Example Logic App workflow:

1. Trigger   daily   on   timer
2. Query   Azure   Cost   API
3. Format   and   email   cost   breakdown   report   to   stakeholders

---

Best Practices for Usage Monitoring

1. **Enable daily exports** to track trends and anomalies.

2. **Tag all resources** at creation; enforce via Azure Policy.

3. **Automate shut down of dev/test resources** outside working hours.

4. **Use budget alerts** and anomaly detection to stay within limits.

5. **Review Azure Advisor recommendations** monthly.

6. **Centralize monitoring with Log Analytics + dashboards**.

7. **Regularly review usage reports** with business and technical leads.

8. **Use forecasting to inform procurement decisions** for Reserved Instances.

9. **Segment usage by environment and department** using tags.

10. **Integrate usage insights with CI/CD workflows** to flag high-cost changes.

Conclusion

Monitoring and analyzing usage in Azure is not just about cost control—it's about enabling smart, sustainable growth. With the right data, tools, and strategies, you can detect inefficiencies, hold teams accountable, forecast more accurately, and ultimately deliver greater value from your cloud investments.

Azure provides the visibility and control necessary to make usage monitoring an integral part of every organization's FinOps practice. In the next section, we'll explore how to further reduce spend through intelligent resource optimization strategies like rightsizing, reserved instances, and eliminating waste.

Rightsizing and Reserved Instances

Rightsizing and reserved instance strategies are among the most effective ways to significantly reduce Azure costs without compromising performance. In cloud environments, it's common to over-provision resources out of caution or to accommodate peak loads, but this often leads to underutilized and idle resources that waste money. Rightsizing is the practice of aligning resource configurations (such as VM size, CPU, memory, and storage) with actual usage, while reserved instances provide substantial discounts in exchange for usage commitment.

This section explores both strategies in depth, including the tools, processes, and best practices required to implement them effectively across various Azure services.

What is Rightsizing?

Rightsizing is the process of evaluating resource utilization and adjusting configurations to better match actual workloads. It helps in:

- Avoiding   over-provisioning

- Reducing   idle   capacity

- Optimizing   cost-to-performance   ratio

Rightsizing applies to:

- Virtual   Machines   (VMs)

- Databases   (SQL,   Cosmos   DB,   PostgreSQL)

- App   Services   and   Kubernetes   nodes

- Managed   disks   and   storage   accounts

Signs You Need to Rightsize

- **Consistently   low   CPU   or   memory   usage** (e.g.,   <20%   utilization)

- **VMs   idle   during   off-hours** (e.g.,   dev/test   environments)

- **Unbalanced resource usage** (e.g., high CPU, low memory or vice versa)

- **Premium services underutilized** (e.g., Premium P1 App Service plans with minimal traffic)

Use **Azure Monitor, Metrics,** and **Log Analytics Workbooks** to identify such inefficiencies.

```
Perf
| where ObjectName == "Processor"
| summarize avg(CounterValue) by bin(TimeGenerated, 1h), Computer
| where avg_CounterValue < 20
```

Rightsizing with Azure Advisor

Azure Advisor provides automated, service-specific rightsizing recommendations:

- Suggested VM sizes
- Low-utilization detection
- Cost savings estimates
- Quick actions for resizing

Navigate to Azure Portal → Azure Advisor → Cost → Right-size or shutdown underutilized VMs

Example Recommendation:

> "VM xyz in resource group rg-dev-eastus has averaged less than 10% CPU usage over the last 30 days. Consider moving to a Standard_B1s VM to save $47/month."

You can apply these recommendations manually or automate with scripting.

Rightsizing Virtual Machines

Steps:

1. Review VM usage metrics over a 30–60 day period.
2. Evaluate CPU, memory, disk IOPS, and network throughput.
3. Use Azure Advisor or Log Analytics for recommendations.
4. Resize VM to a smaller SKU, ideally during maintenance windows.
5. Test application performance after resizing.

```
# Resize a VM using Azure CLI
az vm resize \
 --resource-group myResourceGroup \
 --name myVM \
 --size Standard_B2s
```

Note: Resizing may require stopping the VM temporarily. Always validate compatibility with attached disks and networking components.

Rightsizing Azure SQL Database

Azure SQL offers two pricing models:

- **DTU-based** (Database Transaction Units)

- **vCore-based**

To rightsize:

- Monitor CPU utilization and storage IOPS

- Review Azure SQL Insights and Query Performance metrics

- Use **Elastic Pools** for multiple fluctuating databases

```
# Update performance tier of a SQL DB
az sql db update \
  --resource-group myRG \
  --server myServer \
  --name mydb \
  --edition GeneralPurpose \
  --compute-model Serverless \
  --vcore 2
```

Rightsizing App Services and Kubernetes

App Services:

- Downgrade plans (e.g., from Premium P1v2 to Standard S1)

- Scale in/out instance count

- Review diagnostics and Application Insights data

Kubernetes (AKS):

- Monitor node and pod resource requests/limits

- Resize node pools to appropriate VM SKUs

- Use **Horizontal Pod Autoscaler (HPA)** to adjust replicas dynamically

```
kubectl autoscale deployment myapp --cpu-percent=60 --min=2 --max=10
```

Reserved Instances (RIs)

Reserved Instances provide significant cost savings in exchange for a one-year or three-year commitment to a specific VM family, size, and region.

Benefits:

- Up to **72% cost savings** vs pay-as-you-go

- Predictable billing

- Available for VMs, SQL DB, Cosmos DB, App Services, and more

Types:

- **Azure Reserved VM Instances**

- **SQL Reserved Capacity**

- **Cosmos DB Reserved Capacity**

- **App Service Environment Reserved Instances**

```
# View reservations using CLI
az reservations reservation-order list
```

Purchasing Reserved Instances

1. Analyze your baseline usage over 3–6 months.

2. Identify always-on or steady-state resources.

3. Use Azure Advisor to recommend quantities and sizes.

4. Purchase via Azure Portal or CSP/EA agreement.

Portal Path: Azure Portal → Reservations → Add → Select resource type → Configure

Example:

Reserving 5 Standard_D2s_v4 VMs in East US for 3 years with upfront payment can yield over $5,000 in savings annually.

Exchange and Refund Policies

- You can **exchange** a reservation for another SKU of equal or greater value.

- **Refunds** are available (up to $50,000/year) for unused reservations with restrictions.

- Use **Reservation Utilization reports** to track effectiveness.

Combining Rightsizing with Reservations

The best cost efficiency comes from **first rightsizing**, then **reserving**:

- Step 1: Optimize resource configurations based on current workloads

- Step 2: Lock in savings for those optimized resources via Reserved Instances

- Step 3: Continuously monitor for new opportunities or idle reservations

This hybrid approach ensures maximum ROI from your cloud spend.

Monitoring Reservation Usage

Track usage to ensure you're maximizing commitment:

- Azure Portal: Cost Management → Reservations → Utilization

- Use alerts for underused reservations

- Reassign reservations to different subscriptions if needed

```
# Assign a reservation to a specific subscription
az reservations reservation-order-id update \
  --applied-scope-type Shared \
```

```
--applied-scopes "/subscriptions/<subscription-id>"
```

Best Practices

1. **Monitor resource utilization monthly** using Azure Monitor and Log Analytics.

2. **Use Azure Advisor to identify rightsizing and reservation opportunities.**

3. **Avoid using Premium SKUs unless needed** for performance or SLA.

4. **Consolidate bursty workloads into Elastic Pools or scale sets.**

5. **Prioritize predictable workloads for reservations.**

6. **Tag resources clearly** for usage tracking and reservation planning.

7. **Use Auto-Scale and Serverless offerings** when applicable.

8. **Create budgets and alerts** for teams to drive cost-conscious behavior.

9. **Track RI utilization monthly** and reallocate as necessary.

10. **Document and automate rightsizing reviews** into your FinOps process.

Conclusion

Rightsizing and reserved instances represent two of the most impactful strategies in Azure cost optimization. By tailoring resource configurations to actual needs and committing to long-term usage intelligently, organizations can save thousands of dollars monthly—freeing up budget for innovation rather than infrastructure.

Effective implementation requires continuous monitoring, stakeholder alignment, and integration into operations. The savings, however, are well worth the effort. In the next section, we'll explore budgeting and alerting techniques that help enforce financial discipline across teams and projects.

Budgeting and Alerts

Proactive cloud cost management requires more than just post-facto analysis—it demands **predictive control**. In Azure, **budgeting and alerts** serve as your financial guardrails, helping you stay within your planned expenditure and avoid bill shocks. Whether you're managing a single project or a global enterprise with dozens of subscriptions, setting up budgets and alerts is crucial for aligning cloud costs with financial goals.

This section explores the full capabilities of Azure's budgeting and alerting systems, demonstrates how to implement and automate them, and provides practical best practices for embedding financial discipline across your cloud ecosystem.

Why Budgets Matter

Budgets in Azure allow you to define thresholds for spending at the **subscription**, **resource group**, or **management group** level. When actual or forecasted spending reaches those thresholds, **alerts are triggered**—giving teams the opportunity to act before overspending occurs.

Benefits of budgeting include:

- Enforcing accountability for cost center owners
- Enabling predictive cost control
- Driving cultural cost awareness (FinOps)
- Supporting governance and compliance mandates
- Reducing surprise invoices at the end of the month

Budgeting in Azure Cost Management

Azure Budgets are configured through the **Azure Cost Management + Billing** service and support multiple scopes:

- **Management Group**: Budget across all child subscriptions
- **Subscription**: Budget for entire subscription usage
- **Resource Group**: Budget per project/environment
- **Tag**: Budget per department, application, or owner

Each budget includes:

- **Time period** (monthly, quarterly, annually)

- **Amount** (spending limit)

- **Notifications** (thresholds and contact emails)

```
# Create a monthly budget with 80% and 100% alerts
az consumption budget create \
  --amount 500 \
  --time-grain Monthly \
  --category Cost \
  --name TeamBudget \
  --resource-group dev-resources \
  --start-date 2024-04-01 \
  --end-date 2024-12-31 \
  --notifications actual_greater_than_80_percent="{\"enabled\":true,\"threshold\":80,\"operator\":\"GreaterThan\",\"contactEmails\":[\"teamlead@domain.com\"]}" \
  --notifications actual_greater_than_100_percent="{\"enabled\":true,\"threshold\":100,\"operator\":\"GreaterThan\",\"contactEmails\":[\"finance@domain.com\"]}"
```

Forecasting with Budgets

Budgets in Azure include **forecast-based alerts**, which trigger notifications if the **predicted usage** for the time period is expected to exceed the budget.

This gives you an early warning before costs actually breach the limit.

```
# Enable forecast alert at 90%
"forecast_greater_than_90_percent": {
  "enabled": true,
  "operator": "GreaterThan",
  "threshold": 90,
  "contactEmails": ["cloudops@domain.com"]
}
```

Forecast alerts are calculated using Azure's machine learning models based on historical consumption patterns.

Budgeting Best Practices

1. **Create budgets for every production subscription.**

2. **Define budgets for key resource groups and cost centers.**

3. **Use tags to segment budgets per department or project.**

4. **Set tiered notifications** (e.g., 50%, 75%, 90%, 100%) to warn before breach.

5. **Enable forecast alerts** for proactive visibility.

6. **Review and adjust budgets quarterly** based on actual trends.

7. **Use dashboards and Power BI** to visualize spending versus budgets.

8. **Tie budget notifications to operational workflows** (e.g., pause dev VMs).

Integrating Budgets with Action Groups

Azure Budgets can trigger **Action Groups**, which can be used to:

- Send emails or SMS

- Invoke Azure Functions

- Call webhooks

- Trigger Logic Apps or Azure Automation

This allows automated remediation—e.g., shut down test environments if budget is at risk.

Example: Budget alert triggers Logic App that scales down VM scale sets.

```
# Link budget alert to Action Group (via portal or ARM)
az monitor action-group create \
  --name BudgetActionGroup \
  --resource-group myRG \
  --short-name BudgetAG \
  --email-receivers name=Admin email=admin@domain.com
```

Budget Hierarchies and Inheritance

When managing large organizations:

- Use **management groups** to create umbrella budgets (e.g., $100K/month for all dev environments).

- Subdivide into subscription-level and project-level budgets.

- Inherit policies and tagging rules using **Azure Policy** for consistency.

Budget tracking can be embedded into governance and compliance dashboards for executive reporting.

Alerting Beyond Budgets

Budgets are just one type of alert—Azure provides several complementary alerting mechanisms:

1. Azure Monitor Metrics Alerts

Trigger alerts when usage metrics breach thresholds.

- CPU > 85% for 30 min

- Ingress data > 5GB/hour

- App Service requests > 10,000/minute

```
# Create metric alert
az monitor metrics alert create \
  --name HighCPUAlert \
  --resource-group myRG \
  --scopes
"/subscriptions/xxxx/resourceGroups/myRG/providers/Microsoft.Compute/virtualMachines/myVM" \
  --condition "avg Percentage CPU > 80" \
  --window-size 5m \
  --evaluation-frequency 1m \
  --action-group BudgetActionGroup
```

2. Log Alerts via Log Analytics

Custom alerts based on Kusto queries:

```
AzureDiagnostics
| where Category == "NetworkSecurityGroupRuleCounter"
| summarize TotalFlows=sum(count_) by bin(TimeGenerated, 1h)
```

```
| where TotalFlows > 100000
```

Use cases:

- Detect unusual spikes
- Alert on untagged resources
- Alert when resource creation bypasses policy

Real-World Budgeting Scenarios

Scenario 1: Dev/Test Budget Control

- Budget: $2,000/month
- Thresholds: 80% (warn), 100% (disable CI/CD pipeline)
- Action: Logic App stops unused VMs automatically

Scenario 2: Departmental Showback

- Engineering: $20,000/month
- Marketing: $5,000/month
- Finance: $8,000/month
- Tags used: Department=Engineering etc.
- Power BI dashboards show usage vs budget

Scenario 3: Project Forecasting

- Project Alpha budget: $12,000/month
- Forecast alert triggers at 90%
- Action: Email to project owner + optional scale-down proposal

---

Monitoring and Reviewing Budgets

Use **Azure Cost Management Dashboards** to:

- View daily, monthly, and cumulative spend
- Compare actual vs forecast vs budget
- Filter by tag, region, or resource type
- Export reports for finance or compliance reviews

Review intervals:

- Monthly: All production and cost center budgets
- Quarterly: Annual forecasts, new project budgeting
- Yearly: Departmental financial planning

Common Pitfalls to Avoid

- Setting budgets without actionable alerts
- Failing to review budgets after scale-ups
- Not tagging resources—makes budget segmentation impossible
- Using single global budget instead of layered, scoped budgets
- Relying on alerts without cost control automation

Conclusion

Budgets and alerts are critical components of cost governance in Azure. When configured effectively, they provide early warning signs, prevent runaway costs, and enable teams to take swift corrective action. Whether you're managing one app or a thousand, budgeting ensures that cloud cost management is not reactive—but predictive, proactive, and aligned with business goals.

Combining budgets with real-time alerts, automation, and continuous review gives your organization the ability to grow confidently in the cloud—without losing sight of the bottom line.

Chapter 7: Implementing Modern Architecture Patterns

Microservices with Azure Kubernetes Service

Microservices architecture has become the foundation of modern application design. It involves breaking down applications into independently deployable, loosely coupled services that communicate over lightweight protocols. This approach offers benefits in scalability, fault isolation, technology diversity, and accelerated development cycles.

Azure Kubernetes Service (AKS) is Microsoft's fully managed Kubernetes offering and a powerful platform for orchestrating microservices at scale. This section covers the architectural patterns, design principles, tools, and best practices for building microservices-based applications using AKS.

Microservices Architecture Overview

In a microservices architecture:

- Each service encapsulates a specific business capability.

- Services communicate via APIs (typically HTTP or messaging).

- Teams can develop, deploy, and scale services independently.

- Infrastructure automation, monitoring, and resilience patterns are essential.

Common use cases include:

- E-commerce platforms

- SaaS applications

- FinTech and transactional systems

- Real-time analytics and streaming apps

Why AKS for Microservices?

Azure Kubernetes Service (AKS) simplifies the deployment and management of Kubernetes clusters, letting teams focus on building applications instead of managing infrastructure.

Key benefits:

- **Managed Kubernetes control plane**
- **Integrated monitoring and logging**
- **Scalability and high availability**
- **Support for DevOps and GitOps workflows**
- **Native integration with Azure services (e.g., Azure Monitor, Key Vault)**

AKS is ideal for microservices because it provides:

- **Service discovery and load balancing**
- **Container orchestration**
- **Rolling updates and rollback**
- **Secrets and configuration management**
- **Horizontal auto-scaling**

Designing Microservices for AKS

Microservices in AKS are typically deployed as **Kubernetes Pods**, grouped into **Deployments**, and exposed through **Services**.

Key Design Considerations:

1. **Domain-Driven Design (DDD)** for defining service boundaries.
2. **Stateless services** for scale and resilience.
3. **Data decentralization**—each service manages its own database.
4. **Lightweight communication** (e.g., REST, gRPC, or event-driven).
5. **Centralized logging, distributed tracing, and metrics aggregation.**

6. **CI/CD** **pipelines** for automated testing and deployment.

Deploying Microservices to AKS

Assume a basic architecture with three services: orders, payments, and notifications.

Each microservice is containerized with Docker and deployed via Helm charts or manifests.

```yaml
# sample deployment.yaml for orders service
apiVersion: apps/v1
kind: Deployment
metadata:
  name: orders
spec:
  replicas: 3
  selector:
    matchLabels:
      app: orders
  template:
    metadata:
      labels:
        app: orders
    spec:
      containers:
      - name: orders
        image: myacr.azurecr.io/orders:latest
        ports:
        - containerPort: 80
```

Expose each service using Kubernetes Services:

```yaml
apiVersion: v1
kind: Service
metadata:
  name: orders-service
spec:
  selector:
    app: orders
  ports:
    - protocol: TCP
      port: 80
      targetPort: 80
  type: ClusterIP
```

Use **Ingress Controllers** (e.g., NGINX, AGIC) to route external traffic.

Scaling and Resilience in AKS

AKS supports both **manual and automatic scaling** of microservices:

Horizontal Pod Autoscaler (HPA):

```
kubectl autoscale deployment orders --cpu-percent=60 --min=2 --max=10
```

HPA uses metrics to dynamically adjust the number of pod replicas.

Cluster Autoscaler:

Automatically adds/removes nodes based on pending pods.

```
az aks update \
  --resource-group myRG \
  --name myAKS \
  --enable-cluster-autoscaler \
  --min-count 3 \
  --max-count 10
```

Service Mesh for Microservices

For advanced scenarios, use **Azure-managed Istio (preview)** or **Open Service Mesh (OSM)** to implement:

- Mutual TLS (mTLS)

- Retry and circuit breaker policies

- Service discovery

- Traffic splitting and canary deployments

Example traffic shifting with Istio:

```
spec:
  http:
  - route:
    - destination:
        host: orders
        subset: v1
```

```
    weight: 90
  - destination:
      host: orders
      subset: v2
    weight: 10
```

This supports **safe deployments** and **A/B testing**.

CI/CD for AKS Microservices

Automate builds, testing, and deployment using:

- **GitHub**   **Actions**

- **Azure**   **DevOps**

- **Flux**   **(GitOps)**

Pipeline Example with GitHub Actions:

```yaml
name: Deploy to AKS

on:
  push:
    branches:
      - main

jobs:
  deploy:
    runs-on: ubuntu-latest
    steps:
    - uses: azure/login@v1
      with:
        creds: ${{ secrets.AZURE_CREDENTIALS }}
    - uses: azure/aks-set-context@v1
      with:
        resource-group: myRG
        cluster-name: myAKS
    - name: Deploy app
      run: |
        kubectl apply -f k8s/deployments/orders.yaml
```

Observability and Monitoring

Use **Azure Monitor for containers** to gather:

- Pod-level CPU/memory usage
- Node health
- Deployment failure trends

Integrate with **Prometheus + Grafana** for detailed metrics or **OpenTelemetry** for tracing.

Use **Application Insights** SDKs in each microservice for:

- Request tracking
- Dependency mapping
- Distributed tracing

Securing Microservices in AKS

Security principles for microservices in AKS include:

- **Pod security policies** or Azure Policy for Kubernetes
- **Role-Based Access Control (RBAC)** for API access
- **Azure AD workload identity** for pod-level authentication
- **Secrets management** with Azure Key Vault + CSI driver
- **Image scanning** using Microsoft Defender for Containers

```
# Enable workload identity federation
az aks update --enable-oidc-issuer --enable-workload-identity
```

Challenges and Solutions

Challenge	Solution

Cross-service communication	Use internal services or service mesh
Configuration management	Use ConfigMaps, Secrets, Key Vault integration
Versioning and deployments	Use semantic versioning and blue/green or canary
Data consistency	Embrace eventual consistency, use messaging
Debugging and tracing	Use OpenTelemetry, Application Insights

Real-World Example: E-Commerce Platform

- **Services**: Product catalog, cart, checkout, orders, users
- **Ingress**: Azure Application Gateway Ingress Controller
- **Mesh**: Istio with mTLS and traffic shaping
- **Scaling**: HPA for services, Cluster Autoscaler for nodes
- **Monitoring**: Azure Monitor + Prometheus
- **Secrets**: Azure Key Vault + CSI Driver
- **CI/CD**: GitHub Actions with Helm Charts

Conclusion

Microservices architecture unlocks agility, resilience, and scalability—but it requires the right tools and patterns to succeed. Azure Kubernetes Service provides a powerful foundation to deploy, scale, and operate microservices-based applications with high confidence.

By embracing service mesh, observability, CI/CD automation, and cloud-native security, organizations can build distributed systems that are not only performant but also maintainable and secure. AKS bridges the gap between developer velocity and operational excellence in the era of modern cloud applications.

Serverless with Azure Functions

Serverless computing revolutionizes how developers build and deploy applications by abstracting away server management, offering automatic scaling, and enabling consumption-based billing. **Azure Functions** is Microsoft's event-driven serverless compute platform that enables users to run code on-demand without provisioning or managing infrastructure. It supports a variety of programming languages, integrates seamlessly with Azure services, and provides a highly scalable platform for modern, event-driven architectures.

In this section, we'll explore the architecture, capabilities, use cases, design considerations, and best practices for using Azure Functions to build powerful, cost-efficient, and scalable serverless solutions.

What is Serverless Computing?

Serverless does not mean "no servers." Instead, it means developers don't manage or provision servers. In serverless models:

- Resources are allocated dynamically based on workload demand.

- Billing is based on execution time and resource consumption.

- Scaling is automatic and seamless.

- Infrastructure concerns are abstracted away.

Serverless architectures typically embrace **microservices**, **event-driven patterns**, and **asynchronous workflows**.

Azure Functions Overview

Azure Functions enables you to run small pieces of code (functions) triggered by events such as:

- HTTP requests

- Timer schedules

- Queue messages

- Blob creation

- Event Grid events

- Cosmos DB change feed

Key benefits:

- Event-driven and highly scalable
- Supports C#, JavaScript, Python, Java, PowerShell, and more
- Durable Functions for orchestrating complex workflows
- Deep integration with Azure Storage, Event Hubs, Logic Apps, and more
- CI/CD support via Azure DevOps, GitHub Actions, and more

Function App Architecture

An Azure Function App hosts one or more related functions that share:

- Deployment lifecycle
- Configuration (e.g., connection strings, app settings)
- Compute resources and scale settings

Each function has:

- **Trigger**: What starts the function
- **Bindings**: Declarative I/O connections (input/output)
- **Code**: Business logic

Example: HTTP-triggered Function with Blob output.

```
[FunctionName("UploadToBlob")]
public static async Task<IActionResult> Run(
    [HttpTrigger(AuthorizationLevel.Function, "post", Route = null)] HttpRequest req,
    [Blob("uploads/{rand-guid}.txt", FileAccess.Write)] Stream blobStream,
    ILogger log)
{
    var data = await new StreamReader(req.Body).ReadToEndAsync();
    var bytes = Encoding.UTF8.GetBytes(data);
    await blobStream.WriteAsync(bytes, 0, bytes.Length);
    return new OkObjectResult("Upload successful.");
}
```

Hosting and Pricing Models

Azure Functions supports three primary hosting plans:

Plan	Description
Consumption	Pay-per-use, auto-scaling, ideal for sporadic workloads
Premium	Enhanced performance, VNET support, long-running functions
Dedicated (App Service Plan)	Fixed pricing, reserved compute, used with other App Services

Billing in the **Consumption Plan** is based on:

- Execution   count
- Execution   time   (GB-seconds)

Free tier includes 1 million requests and 400,000 GB-seconds per month.

Trigger Types and Bindings

Azure Functions supports various **trigger types**:

- **HTTP Trigger**:   REST   APIs,   Webhooks
- **Timer Trigger**:   Scheduled   jobs   (cron)
- **Queue Trigger**:   Azure   Storage   queues
- **Event Hub Trigger**:   Real-time   event   ingestion
- **Blob Trigger**:   File   processing   on   blob   upload
- **Cosmos DB Trigger**:   Reacting   to   data   changes

Bindings simplify integration with Azure services:

- Input bindings: Read data into the function
- Output bindings: Write data from the function

Bindings are defined declaratively in function.json or via attributes in code.

Durable Functions

Durable Functions extends Azure Functions with support for:

- Long-running workflows
- Stateful orchestration
- Function chaining and fan-out/fan-in

Durable Functions types:

- **Orchestrator**: Coordinates workflow
- **Activity**: Performs discrete tasks
- **Entity**: Manages state and behavior (Actor model)

Example pattern: Order processing workflow

1. Orchestrator receives new order event
2. Calls activity to validate order
3. Calls activity to process payment
4. Calls activity to send confirmation

```
[FunctionName("OrderWorkflow")]
public static async Task Run(
    [OrchestrationTrigger] IDurableOrchestrationContext context)
{
    var order = context.GetInput<Order>();
    await context.CallActivityAsync("ValidateOrder", order);
    await context.CallActivityAsync("ProcessPayment", order);
    await context.CallActivityAsync("SendConfirmation", order);
}
```

Durable Functions handle retries, state checkpoints, and parallel execution automatically.

Deployment and DevOps

Azure Functions supports modern DevOps workflows:

- **Local development** using Visual Studio or VS Code
- **CI/CD pipelines** with Azure DevOps or GitHub Actions
- **ARM templates or Bicep** for infrastructure provisioning
- **Azure CLI** and **Terraform** support

Example GitHub Actions pipeline:

```
name: Deploy Function App

on:
  push:
    branches: [ main ]

jobs:
  build-and-deploy:
    runs-on: ubuntu-latest
    steps:
    - uses: actions/checkout@v2
    - uses: Azure/functions-action@v1
      with:
        app-name: my-function-app
        package: '.'
        publish-profile: ${{ secrets.AZURE_FUNCTIONAPP_PUBLISH_PROFILE }}
```

Monitoring and Observability

Azure Functions integrates with **Application Insights** to provide:

- Invocation metrics
- Performance and latency tracking

- Exceptions and logging

- Distributed tracing

Use **Live Metrics Stream** for real-time observability during development or incidents.

For deeper insight:

- Export logs to **Log Analytics**

- Correlate telemetry across multiple function apps

- Use **Kusto Query Language (KQL)** for custom dashboards

```
requests
| where cloud_RoleName == "my-function-app"
| summarize avg(duration) by bin(timestamp, 1h)
```

Security and Best Practices

Secure your function apps using:

- **Function keys and authorization levels**

- **Managed identities** for accessing secure resources

- **App Service Environments (ASE)** for VNET isolation

- **Private endpoints** to restrict access

- **Azure API Management** for rate limiting and authentication

- **CORS configuration** for HTTP functions

Use **Azure Key Vault** to manage secrets securely:

```
az functionapp identity assign --name my-function-app --resource-group myRG

az keyvault set-policy \
  --name myKeyVault \
  --object-id <function-app-msi> \
  --secret-permissions get list
```

Common Use Cases

- **RESTful APIs** and backend services
- **Event-driven processing** (e.g., new blob triggers image resize)
- **Scheduled tasks** and maintenance jobs
- **IoT event handling**
- **Serverless integration pipelines** with Event Grid, Logic Apps, Service Bus
- **Real-time notification systems**
- **Lightweight AI/ML inference** at the edge

Challenges and Solutions

Challenge	Solution
Cold starts	Use Premium Plan or Pre-warmed instances
Debugging async flows	Use Durable Functions with built-in tracing
Vendor lock-in	Use open standards (HTTP, Webhooks, Kafka)
Long-running tasks	Offload to Durable Functions or separate workloads
Dependency management	Use layers/packages, minimize external HTTP calls

Conclusion

Azure Functions provides a powerful foundation for serverless application development, allowing teams to build scalable, event-driven systems without the burden of infrastructure management. Whether it's processing files, integrating systems, or powering modern APIs, Azure Functions enables rapid development with minimal overhead.

By leveraging triggers, bindings, durable workflows, CI/CD pipelines, and native Azure integrations, developers can deliver efficient, resilient, and cost-effective solutions tailored to modern cloud-native requirements. As you scale, serverless doesn't just save time—it drives innovation.

Event-Driven Architectures with Event Grid and Service Bus

In modern cloud-native applications, responsiveness, decoupling, and scalability are critical. Event-driven architecture (EDA) enables applications to react to events in real time, allowing for loose coupling between components, asynchronous communication, and improved system resilience. **Azure Event Grid** and **Azure Service Bus** are key messaging services within Azure that support building robust event-driven systems.

This section explores the concepts of event-driven design, the roles of Event Grid and Service Bus, and how to architect event-driven solutions using these technologies. We will examine integration patterns, message routing, delivery guarantees, security practices, and real-world use cases.

Principles of Event-Driven Architecture

In an event-driven system:

- **Events** represent a change in state (e.g., "Order Placed", "File Uploaded").

- **Producers** emit events without knowing who consumes them.

- **Consumers** react to events, performing business logic or further processing.

This design promotes:

- **Asynchronous processing**: Increases throughput and responsiveness.

- **Loose coupling**: Improves maintainability and flexibility.

- **Horizontal scalability**: Each component can scale independently.

- **Real-time behavior**: Enables immediate reaction to changes.

Common patterns include:

- Publish/Subscribe (Pub/Sub)

- Queue-based decoupling

- Event sourcing

- Fan-out/fan-in

Azure Event Grid

Event Grid is a fully managed event routing service that provides support for building event-based applications.

Key Features:

- Push-based delivery with low latency
- Native integration with Azure services
- Built-in retry and dead-lettering
- JSON-encoded events over HTTPS
- Support for custom topics and domains
- Advanced filtering and event subscription

Event Sources:

- Azure Blob Storage
- Azure Resource Manager
- Azure Media Services
- Custom applications
- IoT Hub, Event Hubs, and more

Event Handlers:

- Azure Functions
- Azure Logic Apps
- Webhooks
- Event Hubs
- Azure Service Bus

Example Event Flow:

1. Blob uploaded to a storage account
2. Event Grid publishes an event
3. Azure Function is triggered to process the file

Creating and Using Event Grid

```
# Create custom topic
az eventgrid topic create \
 --resource-group myRG \
 --name orderEvents \
 --location eastus

# Subscribe to the topic
az eventgrid event-subscription create \
 --name notifyBilling \
 --source-resource-id                              "/subscriptions/<sub-
id>/resourceGroups/myRG/providers/Microsoft.EventGrid/topics/orderEvents" \
 --endpoint-type azurefunction \
 --endpoint
"/subscriptions/.../resourceGroups/.../providers/Microsoft.Web/sites/myFuncApp/functions/Bill
ingHandler"
```

Events are schema-compliant with CloudEvents v1.0 and include:

- eventType: Type of event (e.g., "OrderPlaced")
- subject: Resource path or business identifier
- data: Payload
- eventTime: Timestamp

Azure Service Bus

Service Bus is an enterprise-grade message broker supporting advanced messaging patterns and guaranteed delivery.

Features:

- Message queues and publish-subscribe topics
- FIFO and at-least-once delivery
- Dead-letter queues (DLQs)
- Message sessions and transactions
- Scheduled delivery
- Geo-disaster recovery

Service Bus is ideal for:

- Workflow orchestration
- Order processing systems
- Business-to-business messaging
- Any system requiring strict message ordering or durability

Queues vs Topics

Feature	Queue	Topic/Subscription
Delivery Model	One-to-one	One-to-many (Pub/Sub)
Use Case	Point-to-point messaging	Broadcasting to multiple services
Load Distribution	Competing consumers	Parallel consumers

Service Bus with Azure SDK

```
var client = new ServiceBusClient("<connection-string>");
ServiceBusSender sender = client.CreateSender("orders");

await sender.SendMessageAsync(new ServiceBusMessage("Order123"));

ServiceBusProcessor processor = client.CreateProcessor("orders");

processor.ProcessMessageAsync += async args =>
```

```
{
    string body = args.Message.Body.ToString();
    Console.WriteLine($"Received: {body}");
    await args.CompleteMessageAsync(args.Message);
};

await processor.StartProcessingAsync();
```

Event Grid vs Service Bus

Feature	Event Grid	Service Bus
Communication Type	Push	Pull
Target Consumers	Lightweight handlers (Functions)	Enterprise systems (ordering, retries)
Message Type	Events (stateless, lightweight)	Messages (stateful, structured, durable)
Delivery Guarantee	At least once, with retry policy	At least once, FIFO, transactions
Integration	Native Azure services, Webhooks	Business apps, long-running transactions

Use **Event Grid** for **notification-style** architectures and **Service Bus** for **workflow orchestration** or **critical business processing**.

Event Handling Patterns

Fan-Out Pattern (Using Event Grid)

- Trigger multiple handlers from a single event
- Enable extensibility without modifying producers

Queue-Based Load Leveling (Using Service Bus)

- Absorb spikes in demand

- Enable background processing

Event Sourcing

- Record all changes as immutable event logs
- Rebuild system state by replaying events

Chained Events

- Events trigger new events (e.g., "UserRegistered" → "SendWelcomeEmail" → "ProvisionAccount")

Securing Event-Driven Workflows

- Use **Managed Identities** for authentication between services
- Restrict Event Grid endpoints to **private endpoints or IP ranges**
- Use **Key Vault** for secrets and connection strings
- Implement **message encryption** in Service Bus
- Monitor usage with **Azure Monitor and Diagnostics Logs**

Example: Restrict Event Grid subscription to a specific IP range

```
az eventgrid event-subscription update \
 --name mySubscription \
 --ip-filter "203.0.113.0/24"
```

Monitoring and Troubleshooting

- Use **Azure Monitor** and **Log Analytics** to track delivery success/failure
- Enable **dead-lettering** to capture undelivered messages/events
- Use **Azure Diagnostics** for event tracking

Example KQL to view Event Grid errors:

```
AzureDiagnostics
| where ResourceType == "EVENTGRIDTOPICS"
| where Category == "DeliveryFailures"
| summarize count() by bin(TimeGenerated, 1h), StatusCode_s
```

Real-World Scenario: E-Commerce Checkout Pipeline

1. User places an order → Event Grid triggers OrderPlaced event

2. Azure Function handles inventory update

3. Event Grid forwards event to Service Bus topic for fulfillment

4. Subscription triggers payment processing microservice

5. Dead-lettering captures failed payments for manual intervention

6. Final "OrderCompleted" event logs to analytics dashboard

Benefits:

- Scalability via event-driven fan-out

- Fault tolerance with retries and DLQs

- Loose coupling of components for easier maintenance

Conclusion

Event-driven architectures unlock a new level of flexibility, scalability, and resilience in application design. Azure Event Grid and Service Bus offer complementary capabilities to support real-time systems, complex workflows, and mission-critical messaging patterns.

By combining the two, architects can build systems that are responsive, loosely coupled, and future-proof. Whether it's processing IoT events, triggering workflows, or decoupling services, Azure's event-driven foundation provides the power and reliability needed to support dynamic, cloud-native workloads.

CQRS and Event Sourcing in Azure

Command Query Responsibility Segregation (CQRS) and **Event Sourcing** are advanced architectural patterns often used in distributed, high-scale applications where performance, flexibility, and auditability are critical. Azure provides a suite of services—such as Azure Cosmos DB, Azure Event Hubs, Azure Service Bus, Azure Storage, and Azure Functions—that make implementing CQRS and Event Sourcing more achievable than ever.

This section explores these two patterns in depth, illustrates how to implement them using Azure-native services, discusses real-world use cases, and presents best practices for building maintainable, resilient systems at scale.

Understanding CQRS

CQRS separates the responsibilities of reading and writing data:

- **Command side** handles writes (create, update, delete) and focuses on **business logic** **and** **validation**.

- **Query side** handles reads and is optimized for **fast data retrieval and presentation**.

This separation enables:

- Independent scaling of reads and writes

- Optimized data models for each use case

- More maintainable codebases

- Better support for complex domains and rules

Key Principles:

- Use **different** **models** for reading and writing

- Commands are **imperative** and often asynchronous

- Queries are **idempotent,** **side-effect-free,** and fast

- Write and read stores may be **eventually** **consistent**

Understanding Event Sourcing

Event Sourcing stores **state changes as a sequence of events** rather than the latest state. The current state is reconstructed by replaying these events.

Benefits include:

- Full auditability (every change is stored)
- Natural integration with CQRS
- Easier implementation of time travel and replay
- Simplified troubleshooting and debugging

Example:

Instead of storing Balance: $200, store:

- Event 1: AccountCreated
- Event 2: FundsDeposited ($300)
- Event 3: FundsWithdrawn ($100)

State = Replay(events)

CQRS and Event Sourcing in Azure

Azure offers several services to implement CQRS and Event Sourcing:

Responsibility	Azure Service
Command processing	Azure Functions, App Services, Azure API Management
Event publishing	Azure Event Grid, Azure Service Bus, Event Hubs
Event storage	Azure Blob Storage, Cosmos DB, Azure Table Storage
Event replaying	Azure Functions (via Event Grid or Service Bus)
Query materialization	Cosmos DB, SQL Database, Azure Search
Audit and compliance	Log Analytics, Azure Monitor, Diagnostic Settings

Implementing CQRS in Azure

Step 1: Separate Command and Query APIs

Use separate endpoints/services for commands and queries:

- **Commands:** POST /orders/create, PUT /orders/{id}/cancel

- **Queries:** GET /orders/{id}, GET /orders?customer=abc

Step 2: Handle Commands via Functions or API Apps

Use Azure Functions or Azure API Management to receive and validate commands.

```
[FunctionName("CreateOrder")]
public static async Task<IActionResult> Run(
    [HttpTrigger(AuthorizationLevel.Function, "post")] HttpRequest req,
    [ServiceBus("order-events", Connection = "ServiceBusConn")] IAsyncCollector<string>
output,
    ILogger log)
{
    var body = await new StreamReader(req.Body).ReadToEndAsync();
    var order = JsonConvert.DeserializeObject<OrderCommand>(body);
    await output.AddAsync(JsonConvert.SerializeObject(order));
    return new OkResult();
}
```

Implementing Event Sourcing in Azure

Event Store Design

Use **Azure Blob Storage** or **Cosmos DB** to persist events:

- Blob Storage for append-only event logs

- Cosmos DB for structured, indexed, queryable events

Sample event document in Cosmos DB:

```
{
  "id": "event-0001",
  "streamId": "order-123",
  "eventType": "OrderCreated",
  "eventData": {
    "orderId": "order-123",
```

```json
  "customerId": "cust-789",
  "timestamp": "2025-04-24T12:00:00Z"
 },
 "timestamp": "2025-04-24T12:00:00Z"
}
```

Use **partition keys** (e.g., streamId) to improve query and write performance.

Event Publisher and Subscriber Pattern

- Commands write to event store and publish to Event Grid or Service Bus

- Consumers (e.g., billing, fulfillment, email notification services) listen and react to events

```
# Create a Service Bus topic for domain events
az servicebus topic create --name order-events --namespace-name myns --resource-group myRG
```

Use **Azure Functions** with Service Bus triggers to process these events.

```
[FunctionName("SendEmailOnOrderCreated")]
public static void Run(
    [ServiceBusTrigger("order-events", "email-subscription", Connection = "SB_CONN")] string eventMessage,
    ILogger log)
{
    var eventData = JsonConvert.DeserializeObject<OrderCreated>(eventMessage);
    // Send email logic here
}
```

Read Model Projections

Create materialized views in **Cosmos DB**, **SQL Database**, or **Azure Search** optimized for queries.

- These views are **eventually** **consistent**

- Updated via event handlers

- Enable fast lookups, filtering, and pagination

```
[FunctionName("UpdateOrderProjection")]
public static async Task Run(
   [ServiceBusTrigger("order-events", "projection-sub", Connection = "SB_CONN")] string
eventMessage,
   [CosmosDB(
     databaseName: "OrdersDB",
     collectionName: "Orders",
     ConnectionStringSetting = "CosmosDBConn"
   )] IAsyncCollector<OrderProjection> output,
   ILogger log)
{
   var evt = JsonConvert.DeserializeObject<OrderCreated>(eventMessage);
   var projection = new OrderProjection
   {
     OrderId = evt.OrderId,
     CustomerId = evt.CustomerId,
     CreatedAt = evt.Timestamp
   };
   await output.AddAsync(projection);
}
```

Error Handling and Replay

Store failed events in a **dead-letter queue** for manual retry or automated processing.

To **replay events**:

1. Retrieve them from Blob Storage or Cosmos DB

2. Resend to processing endpoints (e.g., via Service Bus)

Ensure your event handlers are **idempotent** to support safe reprocessing.

Versioning and Event Schema Evolution

Plan for:

- Adding new fields (use default values)

- Removing fields (avoid breaking consumers)

- Splitting/merging event types

Use schema registries or eventType and version metadata for flexibility.

Benefits of CQRS + Event Sourcing

- Clear separation of concerns
- High scalability and resilience
- Better performance (reads/writes optimized separately)
- Comprehensive audit log and time-travel debugging
- Natural fit for microservices and DDD

Challenges and Mitigations

Challenge	Mitigation
Complexity	Use templates and libraries to scaffold patterns
Eventual consistency	Handle UI/UX delays, use compensating actions
Schema evolution	Implement versioning and tolerant deserialization
Replay logic	Design for idempotency
Storage growth	Archive events or snapshot state periodically

Real-World Use Case: Financial Transactions System

- **Command services**: Handle incoming transactions
- **Event store**: Cosmos DB with partition key on accountId
- **Event publisher**: Publishes "TransactionCreated", "FundsDebited"
- **Consumers**: Fraud detection, notifications, analytics

- **Read models**: Transaction history for web portal and API
- **Replay tool**: CLI to regenerate state from event logs

Conclusion

CQRS and Event Sourcing are powerful architectural patterns that, when combined, provide a resilient, flexible, and highly auditable foundation for cloud-native applications. Azure makes implementing these patterns feasible with its rich set of managed services that simplify event handling, storage, messaging, and scale-out processing.

By thoughtfully applying these principles and leveraging Azure's tooling, developers can build systems that embrace complexity with clarity—balancing operational rigor with innovation velocity.

Chapter 8: Monitoring, Logging, and Observability

Azure Monitor and Application Insights

Effective monitoring and observability are foundational to running secure, scalable, and resilient cloud applications. In Azure, **Azure Monitor** and **Application Insights** provide powerful tools to collect, analyze, and act on telemetry from applications and infrastructure. These services help detect issues before they affect users, enable root cause analysis, and drive informed decisions about performance optimization and reliability.

This section dives deep into how to leverage Azure Monitor and Application Insights for end-to-end visibility across services, virtual machines, containers, and serverless components. It also covers architectural considerations, integration strategies, and operational best practices for implementing robust observability in Azure-based systems.

What is Azure Monitor?

Azure Monitor is a comprehensive solution for collecting, analyzing, and responding to telemetry from Azure and on-premises environments. It ingests metrics, logs, and traces from a variety of sources, offering a unified monitoring platform for all layers of an application stack.

Core Capabilities:

- **Metrics**: Lightweight numerical data (e.g., CPU usage, request count)

- **Logs**: Detailed, structured/unstructured telemetry (e.g., exceptions, traces)

- **Alerts**: Triggered when conditions in metrics or logs are met

- **Dashboards**: Visualize metrics and KPIs in customizable views

- **Workbooks**: Interactive reports for exploration and correlation

- **Insights**: Specialized views for VMs, containers, applications, etc.

Azure Monitor integrates with **Virtual Machines**, **AKS**, **App Services**, **Azure Functions**, **SQL**, **Storage**, and more.

What is Application Insights?

Application Insights is a feature of Azure Monitor that provides application performance management (APM) and diagnostics.

It enables developers and operators to:

- Automatically detect performance anomalies

- Track requests, dependencies, and exceptions

- Analyze usage patterns

- Diagnose failures and performance bottlenecks

Supported environments:

- ASP.NET and ASP.NET Core

- Java, Node.js, Python, and Go (via SDKs or agents)

- Azure App Services, AKS, and Functions

Instrumenting Applications with Application Insights

Instrumentation can be added in several ways:

1. SDK Integration (for full control and customization)

```
public void ConfigureServices(IServiceCollection services)
{
    services.AddApplicationInsightsTelemetry("your_instrumentation_key");
}
```

2. Agent-Based Monitoring (zero code change)

For App Services and AKS, enable Application Insights via Azure Portal or ARM templates.

```
az webapp config appsettings set --name myapp --resource-group myrg \
--settings "APPINSIGHTS_INSTRUMENTATIONKEY=<key>"
```

3. Auto-Instrumentation for Functions

Azure Functions auto-enable Application Insights with FUNCTIONS_EXTENSION_VERSION.

Use settings like:

- APPINSIGHTS_INSTRUMENTATIONKEY

- APPLICATIONINSIGHTS_CONNECTION_STRING

Telemetry Types and Data Model

Application Insights collects:

- **Requests**: Incoming HTTP(s) calls

- **Dependencies**: Outbound calls (e.g., SQL, HTTP APIs)

- **Exceptions**: Handled and unhandled errors

- **Traces**: Custom logs

- **Metrics**: Custom or system-defined

- **Availability Tests**: Synthetic pings to endpoints

Each item contains:

- Timestamp

- Operation ID (correlation context)

- Cloud role name

- Severity level

- Custom properties

This structured model enables querying across dimensions and deep diagnostics.

Querying Data with Kusto Query Language (KQL)

Azure Monitor and Application Insights use **KQL** for powerful querying and visualization.

Examples:

```
requests
| where duration > 1s
```

```
| summarize avg(duration) by cloud_RoleName, bin(timestamp, 1h)

exceptions
| where outerMessage has "NullReferenceException"
| summarize count() by operation_Name

traces
| where message contains "payment"
| order by timestamp desc
```

Alerts and Anomaly Detection

Azure Monitor supports:

- **Metric Alerts**: Real-time monitoring based on thresholds (e.g., CPU > 90%)

- **Log Alerts**: Query-based alerts from Log Analytics

- **Smart Detection**: AI-driven anomaly detection in Application Insights

Example: Create alert when request failures exceed 5% over 5 minutes.

```
requests
| summarize failureRate = 100.0 * countif(success == "False") / count() by bin(timestamp, 5m)
| where failureRate > 5
```

Alerts can trigger:

- Emails   or   SMS

- Azure   Functions

- Logic   Apps

- ITSM   integrations   (ServiceNow,   PagerDuty)

Workbooks and Dashboards

Azure Monitor Workbooks provide interactive dashboards combining:

- Metrics   charts

- Logs query outputs
- Parameters and filters
- Markdown text

Use workbooks for:

- Application health overview
- SLA compliance monitoring
- Deployment validation
- Security incident investigation

Workbooks can be saved, shared, and versioned within Azure Monitor.

Integrating with DevOps and Incident Management

Observability is most powerful when integrated with development and operations workflows:

- **Azure DevOps Pipelines**: Post-deployment checks based on metrics
- **GitHub Actions**: Trigger rollback if alerts fire
- **ServiceNow/Jira**: Create incidents or tickets from alerts
- **Slack/Teams**: Stream alerts and performance summaries

Use **Log Analytics API** or **Azure Monitor REST API** to automate reports and export telemetry to external systems.

Distributed Tracing and Correlation

Application Insights automatically provides **end-to-end correlation** across services:

- Requests carry operation_Id
- Dependencies and child operations inherit parent ID

- Visualize distributed traces in Application Map

This enables:

- Root cause analysis
- SLA degradation identification
- Performance bottleneck detection

Use **OpenTelemetry SDKs** for standardized tracing across services and cloud providers.

Security and Privacy Considerations

- Redact or encrypt PII before sending telemetry
- Use TelemetryInitializer to filter sensitive data
- Ensure proper retention policies are applied (default 90 days)
- Secure access to Log Analytics using RBAC and Private Links

Example: Redact user emails from telemetry

```
public class EmailRedactor : ITelemetryInitializer
{
    public void Initialize(ITelemetry telemetry)
    {
        if (telemetry.Context.User.Id?.Contains("@") == true)
            telemetry.Context.User.Id = "user@domain.com";
    }
}
```

Best Practices for Monitoring and Observability

1. **Enable monitoring early** in development lifecycle
2. **Instrument both success and failure paths**
3. **Use meaningful names** for telemetry contexts (role names, operation IDs)

4. **Automate alert creation** as part of infrastructure deployment

5. **Segment telemetry by environment** (dev/test/prod)

6. **Avoid over-instrumentation**—focus on what matters

7. **Visualize critical metrics** via dashboards and workbooks

8. **Set alert thresholds based on baselines**, not guesses

9. **Review logs and metrics regularly** as part of incident post-mortems

10. **Leverage AI-driven insights** for early anomaly detection

Conclusion

Azure Monitor and Application Insights provide a mature, extensible observability stack for Azure-based and hybrid applications. With minimal setup, teams can gain real-time insights into system health, application performance, and user behavior. These tools support proactive operations, faster incident response, and data-informed engineering decisions.

By instrumenting applications properly, querying telemetry intelligently, and integrating alerts into DevOps workflows, organizations can build and maintain systems that are not only performant and scalable but also transparent and trustworthy. Observability isn't just about troubleshooting—it's about ensuring confidence in every deployment.

Diagnostic Logs and Alerts

In any cloud-native architecture, visibility into operations is critical. While real-time metrics and application telemetry offer essential insights into the state of running systems, **diagnostic logs** provide the context and detail needed to troubleshoot incidents, understand system behavior, and ensure compliance with operational and security standards. Azure's logging infrastructure, combined with flexible alerting mechanisms, allows organizations to proactively detect anomalies, respond to failures, and enforce observability at scale.

This section explores the structure and sources of diagnostic logs in Azure, how to configure and consume them, and how to create meaningful alerts based on logs. We'll also cover integration patterns, retention strategies, and automation practices that help implement comprehensive logging and alerting systems across diverse Azure environments.

What Are Diagnostic Logs?

Diagnostic logs are structured logs emitted by Azure resources, capturing detailed information about service-level operations, requests, and status changes.

These logs differ from metrics and application-level logs by providing **deep insights into Azure service behavior**.

Types of diagnostic logs include:

- **Activity Logs**: Subscription-level operations (e.g., resource creation, deletion)

- **Resource Logs**: Detailed logs from Azure resources (e.g., NSGs, App Services, Storage, Key Vault)

- **Service-specific Logs**: Custom output depending on resource type (e.g., SQL auditing logs)

Enabling Diagnostic Logs

Diagnostic logging is **not enabled by default** for all services. Configuration is required via:

- Azure Portal

- Azure CLI

- ARM templates

- Bicep or Terraform

```
# Enable diagnostic logs for a storage account
az monitor diagnostic-settings create \
  --resource
"/subscriptions/<id>/resourceGroups/myRG/providers/Microsoft.Storage/storageAccounts/myStorage" \
  --name "storage-logs" \
  --workspace
"/subscriptions/<id>/resourceGroups/myRG/providers/Microsoft.OperationalInsights/workspaces/myLogAnalytics" \
  --logs '[{"category": "StorageRead", "enabled": true}]' \
  --metrics '[{"category": "AllMetrics", "enabled": true}]'
```

Destination options:

- **Log Analytics**: Real-time querying and alerting

- **Event Hub**: Stream to SIEMs or third-party tools
- **Storage Account**: Archival and audit use cases

Log Categories by Azure Resource

Each Azure resource emits logs in **resource-specific categories**:

Resource Type	Log Categories
Storage Account	StorageRead, StorageWrite, StorageDelete
NSG	NetworkSecurityGroupRuleCounter
App Gateway	ApplicationGatewayAccessLog, PerformanceLog, FirewallLog
Key Vault	AuditEvent
Azure SQL DB	SQLSecurityAuditEvents, ExecRequests
App Services	AppServiceHTTPLogs, ConsoleLogs

Check supported categories:

```
az monitor diagnostic-settings categories list \
  --resource
"/subscriptions/<id>/resourceGroups/myRG/providers/Microsoft.Sql/servers/myServer"
```

Consuming Logs with Log Analytics

Once collected, diagnostic logs are accessible via **Log Analytics** and queried using **Kusto Query Language (KQL)**.

Example: App Gateway access log analysis

```
AzureDiagnostics
| where ResourceType == "APPLICATIONGATEWAYS"
| where Category == "ApplicationGatewayAccessLog"
| summarize count() by bin(TimeGenerated, 10m), clientIP_s
```

Example: Blocked traffic by NSG

```
AzureDiagnostics
| where Category == "NetworkSecurityGroupRuleCounter"
| where action_s == "Deny"
| summarize Count = sum(count_s) by bin(TimeGenerated, 5m), ruleName_s
```

These queries power dashboards, alerts, and forensic investigations.

Creating Alerts from Logs

Log-based alerts let you trigger actions when queries return results beyond defined thresholds.

Use cases include:

- Detect failed login attempts

- Trigger alerts on unusual VM reboots

- Monitor for NSG rule violations

- Alert on SQL injection patterns in WAF logs

Create Log Alert via Azure CLI

```
az monitor scheduled-query create \
  --name "HighFailedLogins" \
  --resource-group myRG \
  --scopes
"/subscriptions/<id>/resourceGroups/myRG/providers/Microsoft.OperationalInsights/workspa
ces/myLA" \
  --description "Alert on high login failures" \
  --enabled true \
  --condition "count > 5" \
  --condition-query "SigninLogs | where ResultType == '50074' | summarize count()" \
  --action-groups
"/subscriptions/<id>/resourceGroups/myRG/providers/microsoft.insights/actionGroups/AlertT
eam"
```

Alerts can trigger:

- Email/SMS

- Azure Functions or Logic Apps

- ServiceNow or PagerDuty tickets

Alert Rule Best Practices

1. **Use smart thresholds**: Set dynamic thresholds based on historical data.

2. **Use aggregation windows**: Avoid alert fatigue with appropriate time bins.

3. **Suppress duplicates**: Use alert suppression and deduplication intervals.

4. **Include dimensions**: Filter by region, user, or source IP for context-rich alerts.

5. **Use custom fields**: Attach metadata (e.g., environment, owner) to enrich alert context.

Storing and Retaining Logs

Azure offers flexible log retention strategies:

Destination	Retention Policy	Use Case
Log Analytics	Up to 2 years (configurable)	Real-time analytics, alerts
Storage Account	Up to 365+ days (lifecycle management)	Long-term audit, regulatory
Event Hub	Short-term streaming	Integration with external SIEMs

```
# Set retention for Log Analytics table
az monitor log-analytics workspace data-retention update \
 --workspace-name myLogWorkspace \
 --resource-group myRG \
 --table-name AzureDiagnostics \
 --retention-time 365
```

For compliance (e.g., GDPR, HIPAA, ISO), retain logs for up to 7 years in immutable storage.

Integrating Logs with Third-Party Systems

Use **Event Hub** or **Azure Data Explorer** for integration with:

- Splunk

- Elastic   Stack   (ELK)

- Dynatrace

- SIEM   tools   (QRadar,   SentinelOne)

Set up **Data Export Rules** from Log Analytics to Event Hub:

```
az monitor log-analytics workspace data-export create \
 --workspace-name myWorkspace \
 --resource-group myRG \
 --name exportToSIEM \
 --destination-type EventHub \
 --destination
"/subscriptions/.../resourceGroups/.../providers/Microsoft.EventHub/namespaces/myNS/even
thubs/log-stream" \
 --table-names AzureDiagnostics
```

Automation and Governance

Automate log configurations and alerts via:

- ARM   templates   and   Bicep

- Terraform   modules   (azurerm_monitor_diagnostic_setting)

- Azure   Policy   (audit   and   enforce   diagnostics)

Example: Enforce NSG logs across all RGs

```
{
  "policyRule": {
    "if": {
      "allOf": [
        {
          "field": "type",
          "equals": "Microsoft.Network/networkSecurityGroups"
        },
        {
          "not": {
            "field": "Microsoft.Network/networkSecurityGroups/diagnosticSettings[*].enabled",
```

```
      "equals": "true"
      }
    }
  ]
},
"then": {
  "effect": "audit"
  }
 }
}
```

Real-World Scenario: Healthcare Cloud Deployment

Requirements:

- Log all access to patient data (HIPAA)
- Alert on failed access attempts
- Retain logs for 7 years
- Stream logs to Splunk

Implementation:

- Enable diagnostics for Azure SQL, App Services, and Key Vault
- Store logs in Blob Storage + Log Analytics
- Configure Event Hub streaming to Splunk
- Create alerts on login anomalies, query throttling, and endpoint scans

Benefits:

- Audit compliance with regulatory bodies
- Early detection of malicious activity
- Forensic insights during incident response

Conclusion

Diagnostic logs and alerts are the backbone of effective cloud observability. They provide context-rich, actionable data that allows organizations to understand, secure, and optimize their environments. With Azure's flexible logging and alerting infrastructure, teams can build systems that are not only monitored—but truly observable.

By proactively configuring diagnostics, centralizing log analysis, and using intelligent alerting strategies, you ensure rapid response to anomalies, improve system reliability, and enhance governance. Logging isn't just for compliance—it's for confidence in your operations, architecture, and user experience.

Distributed Tracing and Performance Metrics

In modern cloud applications, especially those based on microservices or event-driven architectures, a single user request can trigger a complex chain of service calls spanning dozens of components. Traditional monitoring techniques often fall short in such environments because they lack the ability to correlate activity across services. This is where **distributed tracing** and **performance metrics** come in—providing visibility into the flow of requests, pinpointing bottlenecks, and helping developers optimize performance and reliability.

This section explores how distributed tracing works in Azure, how to implement and visualize it using Azure Monitor and Application Insights, and how to collect and act on performance metrics. It also covers best practices for integrating tracing into your DevOps lifecycle and ensuring end-to-end observability across your distributed systems.

What is Distributed Tracing?

Distributed tracing is a method of tracking requests as they move through a system composed of multiple services. It helps identify:

- The   path   a   request   takes

- The   time   spent   in   each   service

- Where   errors   or   bottlenecks   occur

Each trace consists of:

- **Trace   ID**:   Unique   identifier   for   the   entire   request

- **Span ID**: Unique identifier for a segment of the request (e.g., one service call)

- **Parent   ID**:   Indicates   hierarchy   of   spans

- **Timestamps   and   durations**

Together, these allow you to reconstruct the entire journey of a request, even if it crosses process, host, or service boundaries.

Why Tracing Matters

Distributed tracing is essential for:

- Diagnosing slow response times
- Debugging errors in complex systems
- Understanding interdependencies
- Supporting SLAs and performance tuning
- Providing business transaction insights (e.g., customer checkout journey)

Without tracing, performance issues often become guesswork. With it, you gain clarity.

Tracing with Azure Monitor and Application Insights

Azure provides native support for distributed tracing through **Application Insights**, part of **Azure Monitor**.

Supported Platforms:

- Azure App Services
- Azure Functions
- Azure Kubernetes Service (AKS)
- Azure Spring Apps
- .NET, Java, Node.js, Python (via SDKs or OpenTelemetry)

Features:

- Automatic trace correlation
- End-to-end transaction diagnostics

- Application   Map   visualizations
- Performance   breakdown   by   dependency

Instrumenting Code for Tracing

In .NET:

```
public class CheckoutService
{
  private readonly TelemetryClient _telemetryClient;

  public CheckoutService(TelemetryClient telemetryClient)
  {
    _telemetryClient = telemetryClient;
  }

  public void ProcessOrder(string orderId)
  {
    var operation = _telemetryClient.StartOperation<RequestTelemetry>("ProcessOrder");
    try
    {
      // business logic
      _telemetryClient.TrackTrace("Order processed", SeverityLevel.Information);
    }
    finally
    {
      _telemetryClient.StopOperation(operation);
    }
  }
}
```

In other platforms, use the respective SDK or OpenTelemetry APIs for consistent trace structure.

OpenTelemetry Support

Azure supports **OpenTelemetry**, an open standard for observability, enabling vendor-neutral tracing.

Benefits:

- Portable across clouds

- Language-agnostic

- Integrates with existing tools (Zipkin, Jaeger, Grafana)

Install OpenTelemetry SDK:

```
npm install @opentelemetry/api @opentelemetry/sdk-node
```

Configure trace export to Application Insights:

```
import { NodeTracerProvider } from '@opentelemetry/sdk-trace-node';
import { AzureMonitorTraceExporter } from '@azure/monitor-opentelemetry-exporter';

const provider = new NodeTracerProvider();
provider.addSpanProcessor(new SimpleSpanProcessor(new AzureMonitorTraceExporter({
  connectionString: process.env.APPLICATIONINSIGHTS_CONNECTION_STRING
}))));
provider.register();
```

Viewing Traces in Application Map

The **Application Map** in Azure Monitor visualizes service dependencies and trace paths.

Features:

- Auto-discovered topology

- Performance metrics (latency, failure rates)

- Drill-down into traces and logs

- Root cause identification

Each node shows average response time, error rate, and call volume.

Custom Metrics Collection

In addition to tracing, collect **custom performance metrics** such as:

- Queue   lengths

- Processing   time

- API   call   latency

- Custom   business   KPIs   (e.g.,   transactions   per   minute)

Send metrics using Application Insights SDK:

```
_telemetryClient.GetMetric("TransactionProcessingTime").TrackValue(125);
```

Or use Azure Monitor REST API to push metrics programmatically.

Metric Alerts and Dashboards

Once metrics are collected, create visualizations and alerts:

- **Metric   charts**   in   Azure   Dashboards

- **Custom   workbooks**   with   drill-downs

- **Alerts**   based   on   thresholds   or   anomalies

Example: Alert if "OrderProcessingTime" > 500ms for 5 minutes

```
az monitor metrics alert create \
  --name "HighOrderLatency" \
  --resource-group myRG \
  --scopes
"/subscriptions/<id>/resourceGroups/myRG/providers/microsoft.insights/components/myAI" \
  --condition "avg TransactionProcessingTime > 500" \
  --description "Order latency exceeds SLA"
```

Integration with Logs and Exceptions

Distributed traces link to:

- **Logs**:   Custom   traces   and   diagnostic   logs

- **Exceptions**:   Stack   traces   and   error   context

- **Requests/Dependencies**: HTTP calls, DB queries, external APIs

This allows unified troubleshooting across data types.

Example KQL query:

```
traces
| where operation_Id == "<trace-id>"
| join kind=inner (
    dependencies
    | where success == "False"
) on operation_Id
```

Performance Bottleneck Analysis

Use distributed tracing to:

- Identify slowest span
- Compare success vs failed traces
- Analyze upstream vs downstream delays
- Detect retry storms or circuit breakers

This helps optimize:

- DB queries
- API latency
- Service mesh overhead
- Dependency timeouts

Real-World Scenario: Retail Microservices Platform

Components:

- Frontend (React, App Service)

- Backend APIs (.NET Core on AKS)
- Payment Gateway (3rd party)
- Database (Cosmos DB)

Setup:

- All services instrumented with Application Insights and OpenTelemetry
- Trace context passed via HTTP headers (Request-Id, traceparent)
- Metrics collected for order latency, checkout failures, cart abandonment

Benefits:

- Application Map visualizes flow from UI to DB
- Traces highlight payment failures
- Alerting detects slowdowns during high traffic

Best Practices

1. **Instrument every service** with consistent tracing IDs
2. **Use correlation IDs** in logs and trace headers
3. **Avoid custom formats**—use OpenTelemetry for interoperability
4. **Monitor trace coverage** to prevent blind spots
5. **Collect meaningful metrics**—not just noise
6. **Use span attributes** to add context (e.g., user ID, region)
7. **Set SLIs/SLOs** based on trace metrics (e.g., P95 latency < 200ms)
8. **Aggregate traces by transaction types**, not just endpoints
9. **Enable long trace retention** for slow/mysterious bugs
10. **Train teams on trace interpretation** and root cause analysis

Conclusion

Distributed tracing and performance metrics are indispensable tools for understanding modern cloud applications. They bring transparency to complex workflows, accelerate debugging, and ensure optimal performance under dynamic load. In Azure, the combination of Application Insights, Azure Monitor, and OpenTelemetry creates a comprehensive observability framework that supports real-time diagnostics, proactive performance tuning, and continuous improvement.

By embedding tracing and metrics throughout your system architecture, you create an intelligent feedback loop—turning every user interaction into insight, every anomaly into opportunity, and every deployment into a measurable step forward.

Chapter 9: Real-World Case Studies and Architecture Blueprints

E-commerce Platform at Scale

Building and operating a high-availability, globally distributed e-commerce platform requires careful architectural decisions to ensure responsiveness, resilience, scalability, and cost-efficiency. Azure provides a comprehensive suite of services that can be combined to design a fault-tolerant, performant e-commerce system that meets modern customer expectations and business demands.

This section presents a complete architecture blueprint for a scalable e-commerce platform on Azure. It walks through the system design, core services, data strategies, performance optimizations, security measures, DevOps integration, and lessons learned from real-world deployments.

Platform Overview

The e-commerce solution supports:

- Product catalog management
- Customer accounts and sessions
- Shopping cart and order processing
- Payment integration
- Inventory and fulfillment
- Notifications and customer support
- Admin analytics dashboard
- Mobile and web client support

The architecture supports:

- Global availability and low latency
- Auto-scaling for traffic surges

- Microservices-based   backend

- Resilient   API   gateway   and   service   mesh

- Near   real-time   telemetry   and   diagnostics

Architectural Components

1. Frontend

- **Web App**: Built using React or Angular, hosted on **Azure App Service** with CDN.

- **Mobile App**: iOS and Android clients using REST APIs or GraphQL.

- **Static Assets**: Delivered via **Azure CDN** backed by **Azure Blob Storage**.

2. API Gateway and Routing

- **Azure API Management (APIM)**: Central entry point for client requests, enforcing rate limits,   auth,   and   request   transformation.

- **Azure Front Door** or **Azure Application Gateway**: Provides global load balancing and   web   application   firewall   (WAF)   protection.

3. Backend Microservices (AKS)

Each microservice runs in **Azure Kubernetes Service (AKS)** and handles a specific domain:

- **Product**   **Service**

- **Cart**   **Service**

- **Checkout**   **Service**

- **Payment**   **Service**

- **User**   **Account**   **Service**

- **Order**   **Service**

- **Inventory**   **Service**

Container images are stored in **Azure Container Registry (ACR)**.

Service Mesh: Istio or Open Service Mesh for secure intra-service communication and observability.

Data and Storage Layer

Service	Purpose
Azure Cosmos DB	Product catalog, shopping cart (low latency, globally distributed)
Azure SQL Database	Transactions, customer orders
Azure Cache for Redis	Session and cart caching
Azure Blob Storage	Product images, customer uploads
Azure Table Storage	Logging, events, static lookup tables

Data replication and geo-redundancy configured for Cosmos DB and SQL for resilience.

Event-Driven and Messaging Architecture

Services:

- **Azure Service Bus**: Order creation → payment processing → fulfillment queue

- **Azure Event Grid**: Trigger post-order workflows (email confirmation, inventory deduction)

- **Azure Functions**: Stateless tasks like sending emails, writing logs, handling webhooks

Example Workflow:

1. Customer places order via Checkout API

2. Order Service emits OrderPlaced event

3. Event Grid routes to:
   - Azure Function → Send confirmation email

- ○ Service Bus topic → Payment Service

4. Upon payment confirmation, Order Service updates status and emits OrderConfirmed

---

Security Architecture

- **Azure Active Directory B2C** for customer login and social authentication

- **OAuth2/JWT** for securing APIs via APIM

- **Managed Identity** for backend services to access Key Vault and databases securely

- **Azure Key Vault** for secrets, certificates, and encryption keys

- **Azure Firewall and NSGs** for network perimeter control

Security logs shipped to **Azure Sentinel** for real-time monitoring and threat detection.

Monitoring and Observability

- **Azure Monitor + Log Analytics** for infrastructure metrics and logs

- **Application Insights** for distributed tracing, availability, and usage telemetry

- **Container Insights** for AKS node and pod health

- **Workbooks** for real-time dashboards (order volume, payment success rate, latency)

Alerts configured on:

- Payment failures

- API error rate spikes

- High order processing time

- Inventory below threshold

DevOps and CI/CD

- **GitHub Actions**: CI/CD pipeline with build, test, and deployment stages
- **Helm**: Package management for Kubernetes deployments
- **Terraform/Bicep**: Infrastructure as code (IaC)
- **Azure DevTest Labs** for isolated QA and staging environments

Pipeline flow:

1. PR triggers build/test workflows
2. Container images pushed to ACR
3. Helm chart deployed to AKS via GitHub Actions
4. Post-deployment smoke tests run
5. Observability tags and deployment metadata tracked

Performance and Scalability

- **Azure Front Door** handles global routing with lowest latency
- **Autoscaling** configured on AKS pods (HPA) and node pools (Cluster Autoscaler)
- **Redis** for reducing DB load and accelerating read access
- **Cosmos DB** provisioned with auto-scale throughput
- **Read replicas** for SQL Database to handle analytical queries

Traffic tests with **Azure Load Testing** validate readiness for peak events (e.g., Black Friday).

Compliance and Reliability

- **Availability Zones** used for AKS and SQL for high availability
- **Daily backups** and point-in-time restore for SQL and Blob
- **RPO/RTO** tested quarterly

- **Compliance** with GDPR, ISO 27001, PCI-DSS via Azure Blueprint templates

Disaster Recovery Plan:

- Failover to secondary region (e.g., East US → Central US)
- DNS and Front Door routing updated automatically
- Cold standby for order fulfillment microservices in DR region

Lessons Learned and Optimizations

- **Avoid monolithic DBs**—microservice independence improves agility and recovery
- **Implement rate limiting** at APIM to protect downstream services
- **Use synthetic monitoring** to simulate critical user journeys 24/7
- **Cache product metadata and availability** aggressively with Redis
- **Test observability during chaos testing**, not just post-mortem

Summary Architecture Diagram (Described)

- Clients connect via Web and Mobile
- Azure Front Door routes to APIM
- APIM forwards to AKS microservices
- Services emit events to Service Bus/Event Grid
- Data stored in Cosmos DB, SQL, Blob
- Telemetry flows into Application Insights and Log Analytics
- CI/CD managed via GitHub Actions, Helm, and Terraform

Conclusion

A scalable e-commerce platform on Azure can meet the rigorous demands of high-traffic, always-on digital commerce by combining microservices, managed data services, event-driven workflows, and robust monitoring. Azure's broad ecosystem ensures resilience, agility, and security from the ground up.

This architecture blueprint provides a starting point for building retail systems that are not only operationally sound but capable of evolving rapidly with changing business needs and user expectations.

SaaS Product Deployment

Deploying a Software as a Service (SaaS) product on Azure demands architectural strategies that support scalability, multi-tenancy, robust identity management, cost efficiency, and operational observability. Azure's rich suite of PaaS offerings, integrated security, and automation tooling make it an ideal platform for SaaS builders.

This section explores the architecture, design patterns, deployment automation, and operational practices used to build and operate a modern, secure, and scalable SaaS platform on Azure. We'll address tenant isolation strategies, identity federation, data partitioning, and continuous delivery pipelines that enable a responsive and reliable SaaS business.

SaaS Platform Requirements

A typical Azure-based SaaS platform must address:

- Multi-tenancy (pooled vs isolated)
- Tenant provisioning and onboarding
- Identity federation with Azure AD and external IdPs
- Scalable web and API tiers
- Data security and tenant data isolation
- Metering, billing, and usage reporting
- Observability and diagnostics
- Self-service and admin portals

Core Architecture Overview

Frontend Layer

- **Web App (React/Angular/Vue)** hosted on **Azure App Service**
- **Static assets** delivered via **Azure CDN**
- **Custom domains** and SSL per tenant (optional)
- Tenant-specific branding (theme engine)

API Layer

- **Azure API Management (APIM)** as a gateway with routing per tenant
- **Azure App Service (Web Apps)** or **Azure Functions** for APIs
- Identity and RBAC enforcement via API policies

Authentication

- **Azure AD B2C** or **Azure AD multi-tenancy**
- Social identity provider federation (e.g., Google, Facebook, LinkedIn)
- Support for SAML and OpenID Connect
- Role-based access control via claims

Multi-Tenancy Design Patterns

There are three primary models for tenant architecture:

Model	Description	Example Use Case
Single-tenant	Dedicated app and data per tenant	Highly regulated industries
Pooled (Shared)	Shared app, shared infra, isolated data (logical)	B2B apps with light tenancy

Hybrid	Shared app, isolated infra for premium tenants	Tiered SaaS pricing model

Azure Resource Groups and Tags are used for tenant grouping and lifecycle tracking.

Data Isolation and Management

Data tier options include:

- **Azure SQL Elastic Pools** for multi-tenant shared databases
- **Cosmos DB** with partition keys per tenant
- **Blob Storage containers per tenant** (private access)
- **Key Vault per tenant** for secrets and certificates

Isolation Strategies:

- Row-level security in SQL
- Separate containers or DBs for regulated tenants
- Tagged resources for cost attribution

Example SQL setup with row-level security:

```
CREATE FUNCTION dbo.fn_tenantAccessPredicate(@TenantId AS INT)
RETURNS TABLE
WITH SCHEMABINDING
AS
RETURN SELECT 1 AS fn_result WHERE @TenantId = SESSION_CONTEXT(N'TenantId');

CREATE SECURITY POLICY TenantPolicy
ADD FILTER PREDICATE dbo.fn_tenantAccessPredicate(TenantId) ON dbo.Orders
WITH (STATE = ON);
```

In application code, set SESSION_CONTEXT based on authenticated user's tenant claim.

Provisioning New Tenants

Provisioning flow:

1. Capture signup details (domain, admin user, tier)

2. Register tenant in a **Tenant Management Database**

3. Deploy tenant resources using **Azure Deployment Scripts** or **Bicep**

4. Update routing, authentication config, and monitoring

```
az deployment group create \
  --name onboardTenantContoso \
  --resource-group tenant-contoso-rg \
  --template-file tenant.bicep \
  --parameters tenantId=contoso plan=standard
```

Use **Azure Event Grid** to notify services about new tenant onboarding for background processing (e.g., send welcome email, assign sandbox resources).

CI/CD and DevOps for SaaS

Use **Azure DevOps Pipelines** or **GitHub Actions** for:

- Code quality checks
- Build and test automation
- Multi-environment deployments (dev/test/prod)
- Tenant onboarding scripts and template deployments
- Versioned API deployment per tenant (if needed)

Pipeline example for tenant provisioning:

```
name: Onboard New Tenant

on:
  workflow_dispatch:
    inputs:
      tenantId:
        required: true
      plan:
        required: true
```

```
jobs:
  provision:
    runs-on: ubuntu-latest
    steps:
    - name: Deploy resources
      run: |
        az deployment group create \
          --resource-group tenant-${{ github.event.inputs.tenantId }}-rg \
          --template-file infra/main.bicep \
          --parameters    tenantId=${{    github.event.inputs.tenantId    }}    plan=${{
github.event.inputs.plan }}
```

Observability and Tenant Analytics

Track per-tenant usage and operational metrics:

- **Custom telemetry via Application Insights**

- **Log Analytics queries filtered by tenant ID**

- **Workbooks** showing active users, API usage, resource consumption

- **Azure Monitor Alerts** with dynamic thresholds per tier

KQL Example:

```
requests
| extend tenantId = tostring(customDimensions.tenantId)
| summarize avg(duration), count() by tenantId, bin(timestamp, 1h)
```

Track tenant resource health via **Resource Graph**, **Service Health**, and **Activity Logs**.

Billing and Usage Metering

For monetization:

- Collect usage metrics (API calls, storage, compute)

- Map to pricing plans

- Generate invoices via **Azure Cost Management APIs** or external tools

Consider integrating with:

- Stripe/Braintree for payments

- Azure Marketplace SaaS offer with metering hooks

- Custom billing engine with webhook callbacks

Security and Compliance

Key practices:

- Use **Managed Identity** for all internal service communication

- Encrypt tenant data at rest (SQL TDE, Cosmos DB)

- Enable **VNET integration** for App Services

- Use **Azure Policy** to enforce naming and tagging conventions

- Enable **Azure Defender** and **Sentinel** for security insights

Tenant audit logging:

- Capture all access to tenant resources

- Export logs to **Azure Storage + Event Hub** for retention and streaming

- Use **Azure Purview** or **Microsoft Defender for Cloud** for compliance

---

Real-World Scenario: B2B SaaS HR Platform

Features:

- Employee onboarding

- Payroll integration

- Leave and attendance tracking

- Org chart and directory

Implementation:

- Shared app infrastructure via App Services and Functions
- Per-tenant database in SQL Elastic Pool
- Row-level security + tenant IDs in JWT claims
- APIM for API gateway and rate-limiting
- CI/CD pipeline that provisions tenant infra and adds them to routing config
- Workbooks for admin usage insights and health metrics

Challenges and Best Practices

Challenge	Solution
Tenant data leakage	Strict row-level security, key vault separation
Versioning APIs	Use API revisions and APIM route mapping
Scaling issues	Elastic pools, autoscaling App Service Plans
Custom branding	Serve tenant-specific configs via CDN or blob manifests
Upgrade safety	Feature flags, canary releases, rollout strategies

Conclusion

Building a SaaS product on Azure offers unmatched flexibility, scalability, and security. Whether you're building a startup MVP or scaling to serve thousands of enterprise customers, Azure's tools support your journey from ideation to global deployment.

By embracing multi-tenancy patterns, automation, telemetry, and governance, your SaaS platform can deliver outstanding user experiences while maintaining operational excellence. A well-architected Azure SaaS platform lays the foundation for sustainable growth, innovation, and competitive differentiation in a dynamic digital marketplace.

Global Enterprise Data Hub

In the age of digital transformation, data is the cornerstone of innovation and decision-making. Enterprises operating across global regions face the challenge of aggregating, processing, securing, and analyzing massive volumes of data in near real-time. A **Global Enterprise Data Hub** on Azure provides a unified architecture for ingesting, storing, processing, and sharing data from distributed systems and applications worldwide.

This section explores how to design and implement a scalable, secure, and high-performance data hub using Azure services. It covers ingestion strategies, data lake architecture, governance models, real-time analytics, and operational best practices tailored for multinational organizations.

Business and Technical Requirements

A global enterprise data hub must:

- Aggregate data from multiple business units, regions, and applications

- Support structured, semi-structured, and unstructured data

- Handle real-time and batch ingestion pipelines

- Comply with data sovereignty and privacy regulations

- Enable secure sharing across internal teams and partners

- Support analytics, machine learning, and reporting workloads

- Integrate with operational dashboards and BI platforms

Core Architectural Components

Ingestion Layer

- **Azure Event Hubs**: For streaming telemetry, logs, and IoT data

- **Azure Data Factory**: For batch ETL from databases, APIs, FTP, SaaS apps

- **Azure IoT Hub**: For ingesting sensor and device data

- **Custom APIs**: For direct client/application uploads

Use **Event Grid** to route and trigger downstream processing for real-time responsiveness.

Storage Layer (Data Lake)

- **Azure Data Lake Storage Gen2 (ADLS)** as the foundation
  - Scalable HDFS-compliant blob storage
  - Fine-grained access control with ACLs and Azure RBAC
  - Optimized for high-throughput analytics
- **Zoned Storage**: Raw → Refined → Curated (bronze, silver, gold)
- **Delta Lake Format** (via Azure Synapse or Databricks) for ACID transactions

```
az storage account create \
 --name mydatalake \
 --resource-group datahub-rg \
 --sku Standard_LRS \
 --kind StorageV2 \
 --hierarchical-namespace true
```

Metadata and Data Governance

- **Azure Purview (Microsoft Purview)**: For unified data cataloging
  - Automates discovery and classification of data assets
  - Enables data lineage and compliance tracking
  - Integrates with Power BI, Synapse, SQL, and third-party systems
- **Tagging and Classification**:
  - Data sensitivity labels (e.g., Confidential, Public)
  - Ownership, source system, last updated metadata
- **Access Management**:
  - RBAC + ACLs on folders and files
  - Purview policies for fine-grained control

Data Processing

Batch Processing

- **Azure Data Factory**: ETL pipelines across regions
- **Azure Synapse Pipelines**: SQL-based integration + transformations

Stream Processing

- **Azure Stream Analytics** or **Azure Databricks Structured Streaming**
  - Join streams with reference data
  - Generate alerts, dashboards, aggregates in real-time
  - Write output to Cosmos DB, SQL, ADLS, Event Hubs

Transformations and Enrichment

- Normalize formats (CSV, JSON, Avro, Parquet)
- Cleanse data (null handling, deduplication)
- Enrich with geolocation, customer segments, and product metadata

---

Analytical and Consumption Layer

Data Warehouse

- **Azure Synapse Analytics (Dedicated/Serverless Pools)**:
  - Query ADLS Gen2 directly
  - Build high-performance data marts
  - Integrate with Power BI, Excel, and ML tools

Business Intelligence

- **Power BI Embedded** for internal portals

- Row-level security for department-specific dashboards
- Custom KPIs and dashboards by geography, brand, or business unit

Machine Learning

- **Azure Machine Learning:**
  - Train models on curated datasets
  - Automate feature engineering and model retraining
  - Deploy models as endpoints for scoring pipelines
- Use **MLflow** or AzureML pipelines for experiment tracking

---

Data Sharing and APIs

- **Azure Data Share**: For controlled sharing with internal/external consumers
  - Supports snapshot and in-place sharing
  - Data usage auditing and termination controls
- **API Layer**: Expose data to apps and partners
  - Use **Azure API Management** to secure and throttle access
  - Integrate OAuth2 and AAD for authentication

Security and Compliance

- **Encryption at rest and in transit**
  - Customer-managed keys (CMKs) via Azure Key Vault
- **Private Endpoints** for storage, Synapse, Key Vault
- **Azure Defender for Cloud** for anomaly detection

- **Geo-redundant Storage (GRS)** with cross-region replication
- **Policy enforcement** via Azure Policy and Blueprints

Data residency considerations:

- Store EU citizen data in West Europe region
- Route US data through East US region
- Use multi-geo ADLS accounts for sovereignty

Monitoring and Observability

- **Azure Monitor** and **Log Analytics**:
  - Track ingestion latency, data freshness, pipeline failures
  - Alert on row count mismatches, schema drift
- **Diagnostic settings**:
  - Enable logging for Storage, Synapse, ADF, Event Hubs
  - Export to Log Analytics or SIEM

KQL Example:

```
AzureDiagnostics
| where Category == "DataFactoryPipelineRuns"
| where Status_s == "Failed"
| summarize count() by PipelineName_s, bin(TimeGenerated, 1h)
```

Deployment and Automation

- Use **Terraform**, **Bicep**, or **ARM templates** to automate provisioning
- **DataOps** practices:
  - Version control for pipelines and notebooks

- CI/CD with GitHub Actions or Azure DevOps
- Parameterized templates for environment replication

Example: Deploy Synapse workspace and link to ADLS

```
resource synapse 'Microsoft.Synapse/workspaces@2021-06-01' = {
  name: 'global-synapse'
  location: 'centralus'
  properties: {
    defaultDataLakeStorage: {
      accountUrl: 'https://mydatalake.dfs.core.windows.net'
      filesystem: 'raw'
    }
  }
}
```

Real-World Case Study: Global Retail Enterprise

Challenge:

- Consolidate sales, inventory, and customer data from 50+ countries
- Enable marketing and supply chain analytics
- Comply with regional data privacy laws

Solution:

- Ingest data via Data Factory and Event Hubs
- Normalize and enrich using Synapse + Databricks
- Store data in ADLS, zone-labeled by stage
- Catalog with Microsoft Purview
- Build dashboards for sales KPIs, churn analysis, and inventory risk
- Apply role-based data access across geos and teams

Outcome:

- Reduced data pipeline latency by 70%

- Enabled 360-degree customer view across global markets

- Improved forecasting accuracy by 25% using ML insights

Conclusion

A Global Enterprise Data Hub built on Azure empowers organizations to unify data assets, deliver insights faster, and operate with transparency and trust. Through a combination of scalable infrastructure, robust governance, real-time capabilities, and intelligent analytics, enterprises can turn data into a strategic differentiator.

As data volumes grow and compliance expectations evolve, a well-architected data hub ensures readiness not only for today's needs but for tomorrow's opportunities. Whether enabling AI, fueling dashboards, or powering new applications, Azure makes enterprise-grade data centralization practical, secure, and future-proof.

Healthcare System with Compliance Needs

In the healthcare industry, managing sensitive patient data while ensuring compliance with regulatory standards such as **HIPAA**, **GDPR**, and other privacy laws is paramount. The design of a healthcare system on Azure requires not only robust infrastructure but also secure data management, strong identity controls, and comprehensive auditing capabilities. Moreover, scalability and performance are critical to handling high-volume patient data, appointment schedules, real-time medical records, and sensitive operational systems.

This section discusses how to design and implement a scalable and secure healthcare system on Azure, focusing on compliance, data privacy, high availability, and fault tolerance. It includes considerations for patient data management, secure storage, API access, compliance enforcement, and reporting.

Business and Technical Requirements

A healthcare system on Azure must meet the following:

- **Compliance**: Adherence to HIPAA, HITECH, and other regional regulations (GDPR, PIPEDA)

- **Data Security**: Protect sensitive personal health information (PHI) using encryption and access controls

- **Scalability**: Handle a growing number of patients, hospitals, and healthcare providers

- **High Availability**: Ensure that critical services are always available

- **Auditability**: Maintain a full audit trail of access and data modifications

- **Real-time Data Processing**: Enable real-time access to patient data across departments

- **Interoperability**: Integrate with other healthcare applications and systems

Core Healthcare Architecture Components

Frontend Layer

- **Web and Mobile Applications**:
    - Patient-facing portals and mobile apps for scheduling, medical records, and appointments.
    - Admin portals for healthcare providers and staff.
    - Hosted on **Azure App Services** with **Azure Front Door** for global load balancing.

Identity Management

- **Azure Active Directory (AAD) for authentication**:
    - **AAD B2C** for patient-facing applications allowing social logins (Google, Facebook, etc.)
    - **AAD P1/P2** for healthcare providers' access to the system
    - **Conditional Access** policies to control access based on risk levels (multi-factor authentication, etc.)

```
# Set up AAD B2C user flow for patient sign-up
az ad b2c policy create \
 --name "PatientSignUp" \
 --type SignUpOrSignIn \
 --user-flow-type LocalAccountSignup \
 --custom-domain patient-portal.com
```

-
- **Role-Based Access Control (RBAC)** for controlling access to specific features, like patient records, appointment scheduling, and administrative functions.

Data Management and Storage Layer

Healthcare data management requires both structured and unstructured data to be efficiently stored, accessed, and processed. Given the high sensitivity of healthcare data, compliance with regulations like HIPAA is critical.

Azure Data Services:

Azure SQL Database: Store structured data such as patient profiles, appointment histories, and billing details. Use **Always Encrypted** for sensitive columns like patient names or Social Security numbers.

```
CREATE TABLE Patients (
PatientID INT PRIMARY KEY,
FirstName NVARCHAR(50) ENCRYPTED WITH (COLUMN_ENCRYPTION_KEY = MyKey),
LastName NVARCHAR(50) ENCRYPTED WITH (COLUMN_ENCRYPTION_KEY = MyKey),
DateOfBirth DATE
);
```

-

Azure Blob Storage: Store unstructured data like medical imaging (e.g., X-rays, MRIs) and patient-generated data (e.g., forms, test results) in a highly scalable and secure environment. Use **Azure Blob Encryption** to ensure data is encrypted at rest.

```
az storage blob upload --container-name patient-records --file /path/to/file --name patient-xray.jpg
```

-
- **Azure Cosmos DB**: Use for high-performance, globally distributed data, particularly for application metadata, session states, and patient telemetry.

Compliance and Security

Data Security

Given the sensitivity of healthcare data, **data security** is paramount. Use the following features to secure the data:

- **Encryption**:

  - **Azure Storage** and **Azure SQL Database** support encryption at rest (Azure Storage Encryption, TDE for SQL).

  - **Azure Key Vault** for managing encryption keys securely, ensuring that only authorized personnel can access sensitive data.

```
# Create a Key Vault and manage keys for data encryption
az keyvault create --name HealthcareKeyVault --resource-group healthcare-rg
az keyvault key create --vault-name HealthcareKeyVault --name PatientDataKey --protection software
```

-
- **Role-Based Access Control (RBAC)** ensures that only authorized healthcare professionals can access sensitive patient data.

- **Network Security**: Implement **Azure Network Security Groups (NSGs)** to restrict inbound/outbound traffic, and use **Azure Firewall** for enhanced perimeter security.

Compliance Framework

- **Azure Policy**: Enforce compliance with data residency laws by ensuring resources are deployed in the correct regions.

Azure Blueprints: Deploy predefined governance models for HIPAA compliance, including resource configurations, policies, and security controls.

```
# Apply Azure Blueprint for HIPAA compliance
az blueprint assignment create \
 --name "HIPAACompliance" \
 --resource-group healthcare-rg \
 --scope "/subscriptions/<subscription-id>"
```

-
- **Audit Logs**: Capture logs for all data accesses and modifications using **Azure Monitor** and **Azure Security Center**. These logs can be exported to **Azure Sentinel** for security analysis.

Real-Time Data Processing

In healthcare systems, real-time processing of patient data, appointments, and clinical events is critical for timely decision-making and operational efficiency. Here's how to manage real-time data workflows:

Azure Event Hubs: Use for streaming real-time data from various healthcare devices (e.g., heart rate monitors, glucose meters) or patient interactions.

```
# Ingest telemetry data from medical devices
az eventhubs eventhub create --name TelemetryStream --resource-group healthcare-rg --namespace-name healthcare-ns
```

-

Azure Stream Analytics: Use to process telemetry data in real time, trigger alerts for abnormal readings, and update records in the database. For instance, trigger alerts when a patient's blood pressure is outside normal ranges.

```
SELECT PatientID, AVG(BloodPressure) as AvgBP
INTO AlertStream
FROM TelemetryStream
GROUP BY PatientID, TumblingWindow(minutes, 5)
HAVING AVG(BloodPressure) > 140
```

-
- **Azure Functions**: Implement serverless functions that respond to changes in patient data or critical conditions and trigger actions such as notifying healthcare providers or updating medical records.

Interoperability and External System Integration

To enhance operational efficiency, healthcare systems often need to integrate with external systems, such as:

- **Electronic Health Record (EHR) Systems**
- **Third-Party Insurance APIs**
- **Public Health Agencies**
- **Pharmacy Systems**

These systems communicate using standard protocols like **HL7** and **FHIR** (Fast Healthcare Interoperability Resources). Azure offers:

- **Azure API Management (APIM)** to expose secure, standardized APIs for third-party integration

- **FHIR Service in Azure Health Data Services** for secure exchange and storage of healthcare   data

- **Logic Apps** for orchestrating complex workflows between internal and external systems

```
# Expose EHR system API securely through APIM
az apim api create --service-name healthcare-apim --api-id ehr-system-api --path "ehr" --display-name "EHR System API"
```

Reporting and Analytics

For generating real-time operational reports and predictive analytics, Azure provides:

Power BI: Integrate patient and healthcare system data with Power BI for dynamic dashboards. Track metrics like hospital bed occupancy, emergency room wait times, and patient   readmission   rates.

 Example: Query patient data and generate KPIs like discharge rates or appointment completion   rates.

```
PatientData
| summarize avg(Age) by Department, TreatmentType
```

-
- **Azure Synapse Analytics**: Use for combining structured and unstructured data for advanced analytics, including predictive modeling for patient outcomes, hospital resource   usage   optimization,   and   more.

Monitoring and Alerting

Monitoring is crucial to detect and respond to issues in real-time:

- **Azure Monitor** for collecting metrics and logs from VMs, databases, and other resources.

- **Application Insights** for end-to-end monitoring of patient portals, API requests, and backend   services.

- **Azure Sentinel** for centralized security operations, threat detection, and response.

Set up alerts based on specific conditions such as:

- Server downtime or degraded performance in critical systems
- Unauthorized access attempts to sensitive records
- High volume of failed login attempts

Deployment and Automation

To ensure a consistent, repeatable deployment process:

Infrastructure as Code: Use **Azure Resource Manager (ARM)** templates, **Bicep**, or **Terraform** to automate the deployment of healthcare resources and ensure compliance.

Example: Automate deployment of a HIPAA-compliant SQL Database.

```
resource sqlDatabase 'Microsoft.Sql/servers/databases@2020-11-01-preview' = {
 name: 'myhealthcaredb'
 properties: {
  sku: {
   name: 'Standard'
  }
 }
}
```

-
- **CI/CD Pipelines**: Use **Azure DevOps** or **GitHub Actions** to automate the deployment of application code and infrastructure updates to different environments (dev, test, production).

Conclusion

Building a healthcare system on Azure that meets compliance requirements and provides real-time data insights involves a combination of secure data storage, robust application design, and seamless integration with external systems. By leveraging Azure's managed services, compliance frameworks, and monitoring tools, healthcare organizations can build resilient, scalable, and secure systems that provide better patient outcomes while ensuring privacy and regulatory compliance.

With Azure, organizations can meet the demands of a rapidly evolving healthcare landscape, ensuring that their systems are not only operational but also future-ready.

Chapter 10: Future Trends and Innovations in Azure Architecture

AI and ML Integration with Azure

As artificial intelligence (AI) and machine learning (ML) continue to evolve, organizations are looking to leverage these technologies to drive innovation, enhance decision-making, and automate processes. Azure provides a rich set of services and tools that allow businesses to integrate AI and ML capabilities into their applications with minimal effort. By utilizing Azure's comprehensive AI and ML ecosystem, businesses can build scalable, intelligent applications that can process and interpret vast amounts of data to derive actionable insights.

In this section, we will explore the different AI and ML services provided by Azure, including how to integrate machine learning models into your applications, the tools available for training and deployment, and best practices for utilizing these services at scale. Additionally, we will look at some of the advanced capabilities of Azure AI, including natural language processing (NLP), computer vision, and conversational AI.

Overview of Azure AI and ML Services

Azure provides a range of services that span the full spectrum of AI and ML capabilities, from simple integrations to complex model development and deployment. Key services include:

1. **Azure Machine Learning**: A cloud-based platform that enables users to build, train, and deploy machine learning models. It offers automated ML, a drag-and-drop interface for model development, and integration with popular libraries like TensorFlow and PyTorch.

2. **Azure Cognitive Services**: A suite of pre-built APIs that allow developers to easily integrate common AI capabilities into their applications. These services include tools for computer vision, speech recognition, text analytics, language understanding, and more.

3. **Azure Databricks**: A unified analytics platform built on Apache Spark, designed to streamline big data processing, collaborative data science, and machine learning workflows.

4. **Azure Synapse Analytics**: A comprehensive analytics service that allows you to run big data and machine learning workloads. It can integrate with both structured and unstructured data sources to perform advanced analytics and ML model training.

These services are designed to be easy to use, with built-in scalability and support for a wide range of use cases. Whether you're building a recommendation engine, performing predictive analytics, or processing large volumes of text data, Azure offers the tools and infrastructure to meet your needs.

Building Machine Learning Models on Azure

Azure Machine Learning (AML) provides a range of tools and services to help data scientists and developers build, train, and deploy machine learning models. Whether you're working with simple regression models or complex deep learning architectures, AML provides the infrastructure and tools necessary for end-to-end machine learning development.

1. Setting Up Azure Machine Learning Workspaces

A **workspace** in Azure Machine Learning is a central place to manage all your machine learning assets, including datasets, models, and experiments. Workspaces allow for collaboration, versioning, and easy management of resources.

```
# Create a new workspace
az ml workspace create --name myworkspace --resource-group myrg --location eastus
```

Once you've created the workspace, you can start creating **experiments** and manage the resources for training and deployment. Workspaces also support **compute clusters**, which enable you to scale your training workloads according to the computational power required.

2. Data Preprocessing and Feature Engineering

Before training machine learning models, it's crucial to perform data preprocessing and feature engineering. Azure provides several tools to help with this:

- **Azure Databricks**: Use Databricks to clean and prepare your data using Spark-based processing, providing a scalable and distributed approach.

- **Azure Data Factory**: For batch-based data transformation and ETL processes, Azure Data Factory can integrate with Azure ML pipelines to automate data workflows.

```python
from pyspark.sql import SparkSession
from pyspark.sql.functions import col

# Create a Spark session
spark = SparkSession.builder.appName('Data Preprocessing').getOrCreate()

# Load dataset and clean missing values
df = spark.read.csv("data.csv", header=True, inferSchema=True)
df = df.na.fill({'age': 0, 'income': 0})
```

Data preprocessing is a key step in ensuring that the model receives clean, meaningful data for training.

3. Model Training

Once the data is ready, it's time to train a model. AML supports various algorithms, including:

- **Regression models**: Linear regression, decision trees

- **Classification models**: Logistic regression, random forests, SVMs

- **Deep learning models**: Using frameworks like TensorFlow, Keras, or PyTorch

- **Automated ML**: Use automated machine learning (AutoML) to train multiple models and select the best one based on your dataset.

```
from azureml.core import Experiment
from azureml.core import Workspace

# Set up the workspace
ws = Workspace.from_config()

# Start an experiment
experiment = Experiment(ws, 'my_experiment')
run = experiment.start_logging()

# Train a model
from sklearn.ensemble import RandomForestClassifier
model = RandomForestClassifier()
model.fit(X_train, y_train)
run.complete()
```

AML provides built-in support for distributed training, which allows you to scale your model training across multiple machines or GPUs.

4. Model Deployment

Once a model is trained and evaluated, the next step is deployment. Azure offers several ways to deploy models:

- **Real-time deployment**: Use **Azure Kubernetes Service (AKS)** to deploy models as real-time prediction services.

- **Batch deployment**: For jobs that process large amounts of data asynchronously, use **Azure Batch AI**.

- **Web services**: Deploy your model as a REST API using **Azure App Service** or **Azure Functions**.

Example of deploying a model to AKS:

```
# Deploy model as a real-time web service
az ml model deploy --name mymodel --model mymodel:1 --deployment-config aci --compute-target aks-cluster
```

Azure Machine Learning provides APIs for monitoring deployed models, scaling up services as necessary, and tracking model performance.

Cognitive Services for Pre-Built AI Capabilities

Azure Cognitive Services provides a wide range of pre-built AI models that can be easily integrated into your applications without the need for extensive ML expertise. These services cover a variety of use cases, such as:

1. **Computer Vision**: Analyze images to identify objects, read text (OCR), or perform facial recognition.

2. **Speech Services**: Convert speech to text and text to speech, or build custom speech models.

3. **Text Analytics**: Extract meaning from text with capabilities like sentiment analysis, key phrase extraction, language detection, and named entity recognition.

4. **Language Understanding (LUIS)**: Build natural language understanding models for conversational AI applications.

These services provide simple REST APIs that you can use to integrate AI capabilities into your applications with minimal code.

```
import azure.cognitiveservices.speech as speechsdk

# Initialize speech recognizer
speech_config = speechsdk.SpeechConfig(subscription="YourSubscriptionKey", region="YourRegion")
speech_recognizer = speechsdk.SpeechRecognizer(speech_config=speech_config)

# Recognize speech from audio file
result = speech_recognizer.recognize_once_from_file("audio.wav")
print(result.text)
```

AI-Powered Applications and Use Cases

AI and ML can be applied across many industries to solve complex problems. Here are a few examples of how businesses can use Azure AI services:

1. Predictive Healthcare

Healthcare providers can leverage AI to predict patient outcomes, recommend treatments, and detect early signs of diseases.

- **Example**: Predictive models to identify patients at risk of readmission based on historical health data.

- **Azure Services**: Azure Machine Learning for model training, Azure Synapse for data processing, and Power BI for insights.

2. Customer Service Automation

AI-powered chatbots and virtual assistants can handle customer inquiries, allowing businesses to provide 24/7 support while reducing operational costs.

- **Example**: A chatbot powered by **Azure Bot Service** and **LUIS** to understand and respond to customer requests.

- **Azure Services**: Cognitive Services for speech recognition, Bot Services, and Azure Functions for business logic.

3. Intelligent Retail

AI can enhance the customer experience in retail by personalizing recommendations, optimizing inventory, and improving demand forecasting.

- **Example**: Real-time inventory tracking and demand prediction using machine learning models.

- **Azure Services**: Azure Machine Learning for training models, Event Hubs for real-time data streaming, and Synapse for analytics.

Advanced AI Capabilities: Natural Language Processing (NLP), Computer Vision, and Conversational AI

Azure provides advanced capabilities in NLP, computer vision, and conversational AI:

- **NLP**: Use **Azure Text Analytics** and **Azure Language Understanding (LUIS)** to build models that can interpret and process human language, allowing you to build applications that can understand user intent.

- **Computer Vision**: Use **Azure Computer Vision API** to analyze images, detect objects, and recognize handwriting. This can be used in scenarios like document scanning, security, and medical imaging.

- **Conversational AI**: **Azure Bot Service** combined with **LUIS** allows you to build intelligent chatbots that can engage with users in natural language, providing real-time support and services.

Conclusion

Azure offers a comprehensive ecosystem of AI and machine learning tools that make it easy for organizations to integrate advanced capabilities into their applications. Whether you're developing custom models with Azure Machine Learning, using pre-built APIs from Cognitive Services, or implementing large-scale analytics with Synapse and Databricks, Azure provides the infrastructure, scalability, and security needed to build intelligent applications.

As AI and ML continue to drive transformation across industries, leveraging Azure's capabilities will enable businesses to stay ahead of the curve, improve operational efficiency, and deliver more personalized and impactful services to their customers.

Edge Computing with Azure IoT

Edge computing is transforming industries by enabling real-time data processing at or near the source of data generation, reducing latency, improving reliability, and optimizing network bandwidth. With the rise of IoT (Internet of Things) devices, more data is being generated at the edge, requiring new approaches to processing and analyzing that data. Azure IoT provides a robust platform to leverage edge computing in your architecture, allowing businesses to harness the power of IoT devices while maintaining operational efficiency and security.

This section explores how Azure IoT facilitates edge computing, how to architect solutions that take advantage of edge processing, and the best practices for deploying, managing, and scaling IoT solutions on Azure.

Understanding Edge Computing in the Context of IoT

In an IoT system, the edge refers to the devices, sensors, and local infrastructure where data is generated and initially processed, before it is sent to the cloud or central servers for further analysis or storage. Edge computing involves performing data computation closer to the data source, rather than relying entirely on centralized cloud servers, providing several key benefits:

1. **Reduced Latency**: By processing data closer to its source, edge computing minimizes the time it takes to analyze and respond to the data, which is crucial for applications like real-time monitoring, autonomous vehicles, or industrial automation.

2. **Bandwidth Efficiency**: Instead of sending all data to the cloud for processing, only relevant or summarized data is transmitted, which reduces bandwidth usage and operational   costs.

3. **Reliability and Resilience**: Edge devices can continue to operate even if cloud connectivity is temporarily lost, providing greater reliability in mission-critical scenarios.

4. **Security**: By processing sensitive data at the edge, organizations can limit exposure of that data to potential security threats on the network, ensuring better control over access   and   compliance   with   privacy   regulations.

In IoT environments, edge computing is crucial for real-time analytics and rapid decision-making, especially in sectors like manufacturing, healthcare, smart cities, and agriculture.

Key Azure Services for Edge Computing

Azure provides a suite of services designed to bring cloud intelligence to the edge and integrate seamlessly with IoT applications. These services enable efficient and scalable edge computing implementations.

1. Azure IoT Edge

Azure IoT Edge is a fully managed service that enables you to run containerized workloads on edge devices. By using IoT Edge, you can extend cloud intelligence to edge devices, such as machines, vehicles, and sensors, for local data processing, machine learning, and automation.

- **Local Processing**: IoT Edge allows for running Azure services (like Azure Stream Analytics, Machine Learning, and Azure Functions) directly on edge devices, enabling real-time decision-making and reducing the dependency on cloud connectivity.

- **Modular Architecture**: IoT Edge uses modules to encapsulate workloads, which can be written in various languages such as Python, Node.js, and .NET, and deployed to edge   devices.

Example of deploying a custom module on Azure IoT Edge:

```
az iot edge module create \
  --device-id myDevice \
  --module-id myModule \
  --hub-name myIoTHub \
```

```
--content-dir ./myModuleContent \
--module-version 1.0 \
--restart-policy always
```

2. Azure IoT Hub

Azure IoT Hub acts as a central messaging hub for secure communication between IoT devices and the cloud. It supports bi-directional communication, allowing devices to send telemetry data to the cloud and receive commands from cloud applications.

IoT Hub is an essential part of any IoT architecture, providing device-to-cloud messaging, device management, and security features such as per-device authentication and encryption.

```
az iot hub device-identity create \
  --device-id device123 \
  --hub-name myIoTHub \
  --status enabled \
  --device-type edge
```

3. Azure Machine Learning on IoT Edge

Azure Machine Learning can be deployed on edge devices using Azure IoT Edge. This allows you to deploy machine learning models directly to edge devices for inferencing, enabling real-time predictions at the source of data generation.

Example of deploying an ML model to an IoT Edge device:

```
az ml model deploy \
  --model-id myModel \
  --deployment-name edgeModelDeployment \
  --edge-target-name myEdgeDevice \
  --region westus2
```

This provides a streamlined way to make predictions and decisions on edge devices without needing to rely on cloud connectivity for inference, reducing latency and bandwidth consumption.

Building a Scalable Edge Computing Architecture with Azure IoT

When designing an edge computing solution using Azure IoT, it is essential to plan for scalability, reliability, and seamless integration between the edge and cloud layers. Here's how to architect a robust, scalable system using Azure IoT services:

1. Data Flow and Processing

The data flow in an edge computing architecture involves three main components:

- **Edge Devices**: IoT sensors, cameras, or machines that generate data.

- **Edge Modules**: Edge computing modules running on IoT Edge devices to process, analyze, and act on the data.

- **Cloud Integration**: Azure IoT Hub facilitates bi-directional communication between the edge and cloud. In the cloud, services like **Azure Stream Analytics**, **Azure Functions**, and **Azure Databricks** are used for data aggregation, storage, and advanced analytics.

A typical data flow in a manufacturing scenario might look like this:

1. IoT sensors on machines send telemetry data (e.g., temperature, vibration) to IoT Edge devices.

2. The edge devices process the data locally using Azure IoT Edge modules (e.g., anomaly detection algorithms).

3. If certain thresholds are exceeded, the device sends the data to the cloud for deeper analysis using Azure IoT Hub.

4. In the cloud, real-time insights and alerts are generated and sent to the factory management system.

2. Edge Computing Scenarios

Here are several use cases that demonstrate how edge computing enhances performance and reduces latency in real-world applications:

A. Industrial IoT (IIoT)

In industrial settings, edge computing can improve operational efficiency by monitoring and controlling machines in real-time. Sensors on factory floors can detect issues before they cause machine downtime, allowing for predictive maintenance.

For example, using **Azure IoT Edge** to monitor equipment conditions, the edge device can make decisions, like stopping a machine that is operating outside of safe parameters, without needing to wait for cloud processing.

B. Smart Cities

Smart city applications, such as traffic management and waste monitoring, can benefit from edge computing by processing data locally. Traffic cameras or sensors can analyze traffic patterns and make real-time adjustments to traffic lights without relying on the cloud, ensuring better traffic flow and reducing delays.

C. Healthcare

Edge devices in hospitals, like wearable patient monitors, can immediately alert healthcare providers if a patient's vitals fall outside of normal ranges. By processing the data locally, the system reduces the reliance on cloud infrastructure for time-sensitive decisions.

3. Scaling Edge Solutions

As IoT devices scale in an edge computing solution, managing hundreds or thousands of devices becomes a challenge. Azure IoT simplifies this with several scalability features:

- **Device Groups**: Devices can be organized into groups to apply configuration changes and software updates uniformly.

- **IoT Edge Modules**: With modular architecture, IoT Edge modules can be scaled up or down depending on the application's computational needs.

- **Auto-scaling**: IoT Hub and IoT Edge services can automatically scale based on workload demands, ensuring resources are allocated as needed.

4. Security at the Edge

Security is a critical aspect of edge computing, as IoT devices are often exposed to the internet and can be vulnerable to attacks. Azure IoT Edge provides several built-in security features:

- **Device Authentication**: Devices are authenticated using **X.509 certificates** and symmetric keys, ensuring secure communication between edge devices and IoT Hub.

- **Data Encryption**: Data in transit and at rest is encrypted using industry-standard protocols.

- **Secure Boot**: IoT Edge devices can be configured to boot securely, ensuring that only authenticated and authorized code is executed.

```
# Enable secure boot for IoT Edge device
az iot edge device create \
 --device-id mydevice \
 --hub-name myIoTHub \
 --secure-boot-enabled true
```

Best Practices for Edge Computing with Azure IoT

1. **Device Management**: Leverage **Azure IoT Hub**'s device management capabilities to ensure that devices are configured correctly, updated regularly, and secure.

2. **Local Data Processing**: Minimize latency by processing as much data as possible at the edge, sending only essential data to the cloud.

3. **Efficient Networking**: Use **IoT Edge** to compress and preprocess data before sending it to the cloud, reducing network load and bandwidth consumption.

4. **Failover and Resilience**: Design edge applications to function even during intermittent or complete cloud outages. Ensure that edge devices can continue processing and make decisions autonomously.

5. **Scalable Infrastructure**: Use **Azure Kubernetes Service (AKS)** for managing containerized workloads in IoT Edge environments, allowing for scalability and easier management of edge device clusters.

Conclusion

Azure IoT offers a powerful platform for building edge computing solutions that can handle real-time data processing and intelligent decision-making at the edge. By leveraging services such as **Azure IoT Edge**, **Azure IoT Hub**, and **Azure Machine Learning**, organizations can build scalable, resilient, and secure edge computing solutions that improve performance, reduce latency, and enhance operational efficiency.

Edge computing will continue to play a critical role in industries such as manufacturing, healthcare, smart cities, and transportation, where real-time data processing and low latency are essential. With Azure's capabilities, businesses can embrace edge computing and unlock new opportunities for automation, intelligence, and innovation across their operations.

Sustainable Cloud Practices

As organizations move their operations to the cloud, the need for sustainable cloud practices has become increasingly important. Cloud services, especially those as extensive and scalable as Azure, offer immense advantages in terms of flexibility, performance, and cost-efficiency. However, these benefits also come with a significant environmental footprint, particularly concerning energy consumption, carbon emissions, and electronic waste.

Azure, along with other major cloud providers, is making significant strides in reducing its environmental impact through innovations in renewable energy, resource optimization, and green computing initiatives. This section explores the concept of sustainable cloud computing, the environmental impact of cloud infrastructures, and how Azure provides tools and strategies to help organizations achieve their sustainability goals while maintaining high performance and efficiency.

Understanding the Environmental Impact of Cloud Computing

The environmental impact of cloud computing primarily stems from the following factors:

1. **Energy Consumption**: Data centers that run cloud services consume significant amounts of electricity, especially for running servers, networking equipment, and cooling systems.

2. **Carbon Emissions**: The majority of data centers are powered by non-renewable energy sources, contributing to global carbon emissions.

3. **Electronic Waste**: The rapid pace of technological advancement in data centers results in frequent hardware upgrades, contributing to electronic waste.

4. **Water Usage**: Cooling systems used in data centers often require large amounts of water, impacting local water resources.

To combat these environmental impacts, the cloud computing industry has been focusing on more sustainable practices, such as using renewable energy sources, improving energy efficiency, and managing electronic waste. Azure, for instance, has set ambitious goals to become carbon-neutral and improve energy efficiency across its global data centers.

Azure's Commitment to Sustainability

Microsoft Azure has set ambitious sustainability goals aimed at reducing the environmental footprint of its cloud services. These include:

1. **Carbon Neutrality**: Microsoft has pledged to be carbon-neutral by 2030. By 2025, Microsoft aims to have reduced the carbon emissions of its data centers by 30%. Furthermore, the company has committed to eliminating its historical carbon footprint by 2050.

2. **Renewable Energy**: Azure data centers are increasingly powered by renewable energy sources such as wind, solar, and hydroelectric power. As of 2020, Azure's data centers are already powered by 60% renewable energy, and Microsoft plans to increase that figure to 100% in the coming years.

3. **Sustainable Data Centers**: Azure is focused on building energy-efficient data centers that optimize power usage and reduce energy consumption per server. Additionally, the company is exploring innovative cooling techniques such as using ambient air for cooling and utilizing natural resources for sustainable energy sources.

4. **Waste Reduction**: Azure data centers adhere to strict waste management protocols, recycling electronic waste, and repurposing hardware when possible. Microsoft is committed to reusing materials and ensuring that its data centers adhere to the highest standards of environmental protection.

Tools for Measuring and Optimizing Sustainability on Azure

Azure provides several tools and services that allow organizations to measure and optimize their sustainability efforts. These tools help businesses track energy consumption, carbon emissions, and resource utilization to ensure they are meeting their sustainability goals.

1. Azure Sustainability Calculator

The **Azure Sustainability Calculator** is a tool designed to help organizations measure the environmental impact of their cloud workloads. This tool provides detailed insights into carbon emissions and energy usage, giving organizations the ability to assess their environmental footprint and optimize their cloud resource consumption.

- **Carbon Footprint Estimation**: The Sustainability Calculator estimates the amount of carbon emissions associated with using specific Azure services.

- **Energy Efficiency Recommendations**: The tool provides suggestions for optimizing resource usage to reduce energy consumption, such as scaling down underutilized resources, using serverless services, and leveraging auto-scaling features.

- **Regional Insights**: Users can view their carbon impact by region, enabling them to make more informed decisions about where to host their workloads based on the environmental performance of Azure data centers.

To use the Sustainability Calculator, organizations can provide details about their Azure subscriptions and workloads, and the tool will generate a detailed report showing carbon emissions associated with their cloud usage.

2. Azure Resource Manager and Power Efficiency

Azure provides several features to help customers optimize the power efficiency of their cloud workloads. Through **Azure Resource Manager (ARM)**, users can implement resource provisioning strategies that reduce energy consumption while maintaining performance.

- **Resource Scheduling**: By utilizing ARM templates, organizations can automate the shutdown of non-essential resources during off-hours, such as development and testing environments, reducing energy consumption when they are not in use.

```json
{
  "$schema": "https://schema.management.azure.com/schemas/2019-04-01/deploymentTemplate.json#",
  "contentVersion": "1.0.0.0",
  "resources": [
    {
      "type": "Microsoft.Compute/virtualMachines",
```

```
    "apiVersion": "2020-06-01",
    "location": "eastus",
    "properties": {
      "hardwareProfile": {
        "vmSize": "Standard_B1ms"
      },
      "osProfile": {
        "computerName": "vm-shutdown-example",
        "adminUsername": "admin",
        "adminPassword": "P@ssw0rd"
      }
    }
  }
 ]
}
```

- **Auto-Scaling**: Azure provides built-in auto-scaling features for virtual machines, app services, and containers, enabling the system to automatically adjust resource allocation based on workload demand. This ensures that resources are only consumed when needed, reducing idle times and optimizing energy use.

Green Development Practices in Azure

While Azure provides the infrastructure and tools for sustainability, developers also play a significant role in optimizing the energy efficiency of applications. Here are some green development practices that can be implemented in an Azure-based environment:

1. Efficient Code Practices

Efficient code directly translates to lower resource consumption and energy savings. Developers should focus on writing efficient, optimized code that reduces the computational power required to run applications. Some practices include:

- **Optimizing algorithms** to reduce processing time.

- **Reducing unnecessary data processing** to avoid wasteful computation.

- **Using caching** to minimize the need for repeated calculations.

2. Serverless Architecture

Serverless computing, such as **Azure Functions** and **Azure Logic Apps**, allows developers to build applications that automatically scale based on demand. With serverless computing, resources are provisioned dynamically and only used when needed, leading to more efficient resource usage.

- **Azure Functions**: A serverless compute service that runs code in response to events and triggers, automatically scaling up or down based on usage. This eliminates the need for constantly running virtual machines, which can significantly reduce energy consumption.

```
az functionapp plan create --name "FunctionPlan" --resource-group "ResourceGroup" --sku Consumption
```

- **Azure Logic Apps**: Automate workflows and integrate services without provisioning servers. By running only when triggered, Logic Apps minimize resource consumption, contributing to a more sustainable application architecture.

3. Containerization and Kubernetes

Azure Kubernetes Service (AKS) provides a scalable platform for running containerized applications. Containers are lightweight and more efficient than traditional virtual machines, leading to better resource utilization.

- **Efficient Container Scheduling**: AKS can automatically schedule containers based on resource demand, ensuring that workloads are distributed efficiently across the available nodes. By optimizing resource allocation, containers help reduce waste and improve energy efficiency.

```
kubectl apply -f deployment.yaml
```

- **Container Auto-Scaling**: AKS supports horizontal pod auto-scaling, which automatically adjusts the number of pods based on the load. This ensures that resources are dynamically allocated and deallocated, improving efficiency.

Case Study: Sustainable Healthcare Solution

A healthcare organization moving its data processing to Azure wanted to reduce its environmental footprint while maintaining high performance. The company adopted several sustainable practices:

- **Energy-Efficient Data Processing**: Using **Azure Databricks** to process patient data in an optimized way, reducing the energy consumption associated with traditional processing   methods.

- **Serverless Compute**: The organization migrated its microservices to **Azure Functions**, ensuring that resources were used only when necessary, eliminating the need   for   always-on   virtual   machines.

- **Carbon-Neutral Hosting**: By choosing to deploy its applications in regions powered by 100% renewable energy, the company significantly reduced its carbon emissions.

As a result, the organization was able to reduce its carbon emissions by 40% while still achieving the required performance and scalability for its applications.

Conclusion

Sustainable cloud practices are essential for mitigating the environmental impact of cloud computing, and Azure offers a wide array of tools and services that support energy-efficient, carbon-conscious operations. By leveraging Azure's sustainability features, adopting energy-efficient development practices, and optimizing resource usage, organizations can reduce their carbon footprint while maintaining high levels of performance and scalability.

As the world moves toward more sustainable practices, cloud computing platforms like Azure are at the forefront of driving the adoption of green technologies and solutions. Through continued innovation in energy efficiency and sustainability, Azure is empowering businesses to build the future of computing without compromising the planet.

The Role of DevOps in Modern Architectures

In today's fast-paced software development environment, **DevOps** has become an essential practice for organizations looking to increase development velocity, enhance collaboration, and improve the reliability and scalability of their applications. DevOps is a cultural shift that integrates development (Dev) and operations (Ops) teams to automate the entire software delivery lifecycle. This approach focuses on collaboration, continuous integration and delivery (CI/CD), automation, monitoring, and rapid feedback loops.

In this section, we will explore the role of DevOps in modern cloud architectures, particularly in Azure environments. We will discuss how DevOps enables organizations to efficiently build, test, deploy, and maintain applications, while leveraging the power of Azure's suite of services. We will also cover best practices for implementing DevOps principles, the tools and technologies involved, and how DevOps can lead to better business outcomes.

DevOps Principles in Modern Architectures

DevOps is not just a set of tools but a cultural shift aimed at improving collaboration between development and operations teams. It is built on several key principles:

1. **Collaboration and Communication**: DevOps emphasizes the importance of collaboration between developers, IT operations, and other stakeholders. This means breaking down silos, fostering open communication, and encouraging teams to work together throughout the entire software development lifecycle.

2. **Automation**: One of the core tenets of DevOps is automation. By automating repetitive tasks such as code integration, deployment, testing, and infrastructure provisioning, teams can focus on more strategic activities, reduce human error, and accelerate delivery.

3. **Continuous Integration (CI)**: In CI, developers frequently commit their code to a shared repository, where automated builds and tests are run to ensure that new code changes do not break existing functionality. This approach helps catch issues early in the development process and ensures the application is always in a deployable state.

4. **Continuous Delivery (CD)**: CD extends the principles of CI by automating the deployment of code changes to staging or production environments. This enables teams to release updates to end-users more frequently and with greater confidence.

5. **Monitoring and Feedback**: DevOps promotes the use of monitoring tools to track application performance, infrastructure health, and user behavior. This real-time feedback loop allows teams to quickly detect and address issues, ensuring that the system is always running optimally.

DevOps and Azure: A Perfect Match

Azure provides a powerful set of tools and services to implement DevOps practices, making it easier for organizations to build, test, deploy, and maintain cloud-native applications. Azure DevOps, combined with other Azure services, enables teams to automate their workflows and accelerate the software delivery pipeline.

1. Azure DevOps Services

Azure DevOps is a set of development tools that provide a complete DevOps lifecycle management solution. It includes services such as:

- **Azure Repos**: A version control system that supports Git and Team Foundation Version Control (TFVC). It allows teams to collaborate on code changes, manage branches, and track code history.

```
# Clone a repository from Azure Repos
git clone https://dev.azure.com/myorg/myproject/_git/myrepo
```

- **Azure Pipelines**: A CI/CD service that automates the build, test, and deployment of applications. It supports a wide range of programming languages and platforms and integrates with various source control systems. With Azure Pipelines, teams can easily set up continuous integration and continuous delivery pipelines to automatically build, test, and deploy code changes to multiple environments.

```yaml
# Azure Pipeline YAML definition for a .NET Core application
trigger:
- main

pool:
  vmImage: 'ubuntu-latest'

steps:
- task: UseDotNet@2
  inputs:
    packageType: 'sdk'
    version: '5.x'
    installationPath: $(Agent.ToolsDirectory)/dotnet

- task: DotNetCoreCLI@2
  inputs:
    command: 'restore'
    projects: '**/*.csproj'

- task: DotNetCoreCLI@2
  inputs:
    command: 'build'
    projects: '**/*.csproj'

- task: DotNetCoreCLI@2
  inputs:
    command: 'publish'
    publishWebProjects: true
    arguments: '--configuration Release --output $(Build.ArtifactStagingDirectory)'
    zipAfterPublish: true
```

- **Azure Artifacts**: A package management service that allows teams to host and share packages, such as NuGet, npm, or Maven, within Azure DevOps. It simplifies dependency management and ensures consistency across development environments.

- **Azure Test Plans**: A tool for managing test cases, running automated tests, and tracking test results. Azure Test Plans helps teams ensure that the software is tested thoroughly and that issues are identified early in the development process.

2. Infrastructure as Code (IaC)

Infrastructure as Code (IaC) is a key concept in DevOps, allowing teams to define and manage their infrastructure through code. This approach ensures consistency and repeatability in provisioning and managing cloud resources.

Azure offers several tools for implementing IaC:

- **Azure Resource Manager (ARM) Templates**: ARM templates are JSON files that describe the infrastructure resources and their configurations. These templates allow teams to automate the deployment of Azure resources in a consistent and reproducible manner.

```json
{
  "$schema": "https://schema.management.azure.com/schemas/2019-04-01/deploymentTemplate.json#",
  "contentVersion": "1.0.0.0",
  "resources": [
    {
      "type": "Microsoft.Compute/virtualMachines",
      "apiVersion": "2021-03-01",
      "location": "East US",
      "properties": {
        "hardwareProfile": {
          "vmSize": "Standard_B1ms"
        },
        "osProfile": {
          "computerName": "myvm",
          "adminUsername": "adminuser",
          "adminPassword": "P@ssw0rd"
        }
      }
    }
  ]
}
```

- **Bicep**: A simplified, more readable alternative to ARM templates, Bicep allows you to define Azure resources in a declarative syntax. It compiles to ARM templates behind the scenes, providing the same benefits with less verbosity.

```bicep
resource vm 'Microsoft.Compute/virtualMachines@2021-03-01' = {
  name: 'myVM'
  location: 'East US'
```

```
 properties: {
  hardwareProfile: {
   vmSize: 'Standard_B1ms'
  }
  osProfile: {
   computerName: 'myvm'
   adminUsername: 'adminuser'
   adminPassword: 'P@ssw0rd'
  }
 }
}
```

- **Terraform**: An open-source IaC tool that allows you to define and provision cloud infrastructure across a variety of providers, including Azure. Terraform provides a declarative syntax for managing resources and can be used to automate the setup of Azure   environments.

```
provider "azurerm" {
 features {}
}

resource "azurerm_virtual_machine" "example" {
 name               = "example-vm"
 location           = "East US"
 resource_group_name = azurerm_resource_group.example.name
 network_interface_ids = [azurerm_network_interface.example.id]
 vm_size            = "Standard_B1ms"

 os_profile {
  computer_name  = "hostname"
  admin_username = "adminuser"
  admin_password = "P@ssw0rd"
 }

 os_profile_windows_config {
  provision_vm_agent = true
  enable_automatic_upgrades = true
 }
}
```

3. Monitoring and Feedback with Azure

Effective monitoring is critical to DevOps success, as it provides real-time insights into application performance, infrastructure health, and user behavior. Azure offers several tools for monitoring and feedback that integrate seamlessly with DevOps pipelines:

- **Azure Monitor**: A comprehensive service for monitoring applications and infrastructure. It collects data from various sources, including virtual machines, containers, and web apps, and provides insights through dashboards and alerts.

- **Application Insights**: Part of Azure Monitor, Application Insights provides real-time monitoring of applications, including application performance, error tracking, and user behavior analytics. It is particularly useful for identifying issues early in the development   cycle.

```
# Create an Application Insights resource
az monitor app-insights component create --app myAppInsights --resource-group myResourceGroup --location eastus
```

- **Azure Log Analytics**: A tool that collects and analyzes log data from multiple sources, providing detailed insights into resource usage, application errors, and security events. Log Analytics allows teams to write custom queries to explore data and generate actionable   insights.

DevOps Culture: Collaboration and Continuous Improvement

At the heart of DevOps lies a culture of collaboration and continuous improvement. DevOps practices break down traditional silos between development, operations, and other stakeholders, fostering a more collaborative and agile work environment. Key cultural elements include:

1. **Collaboration**: Teams are encouraged to collaborate early and often. Developers work closely with operations teams to understand system constraints and operational requirements.

2. **Automation**: Automation is at the core of DevOps, eliminating repetitive tasks and reducing the potential for human error. This leads to faster delivery cycles and more reliable   systems.

3. **Continuous Improvement**: DevOps encourages a mindset of constant improvement. Teams regularly review their processes, identify bottlenecks, and experiment with new tools   and   practices   to   improve   efficiency.

4. **Ownership**: Developers and operations teams share responsibility for the application lifecycle. This means that developers are responsible for the deployment and maintenance of the applications they build, ensuring better collaboration and accountability.

Conclusion

DevOps has become an essential practice for modern software development, enabling organizations to release software faster, with higher quality, and at a lower cost. By leveraging the power of Azure DevOps and Azure's suite of cloud services, organizations can streamline their software delivery pipelines, automate infrastructure provisioning, and monitor application performance in real-time. The key to DevOps success lies not just in the tools and automation, but also in fostering a culture of collaboration, continuous improvement, and shared responsibility across teams.

As DevOps continues to evolve, its role in driving business agility, innovation, and operational efficiency will only become more important. With Azure's robust DevOps capabilities, organizations can stay ahead of the competition, delivering high-quality software quickly and reliably while meeting the demands of modern cloud architectures.

Chapter 11: Appendices

Glossary of Terms

In this section, we provide a comprehensive glossary of terms commonly used in cloud computing, Azure, and related technologies. This glossary serves as a reference for readers to quickly understand the key concepts and terminology that appear throughout the book. Understanding these terms will help you navigate the intricacies of Azure architecture and cloud computing principles more effectively.

A

API   (Application   Programming   Interface)
A set of protocols and tools that allow different software applications to communicate with each other. APIs enable integration between systems, allowing developers to access specific functionality or data from external services.

App   Service
A platform-as-a-service (PaaS) offering from Azure that allows developers to host web applications, REST APIs, and mobile backends. It provides a fully managed environment for building, deploying, and scaling applications.

Availability   Zone
A physically separate location within an Azure region that has its own power, cooling, and networking. Availability Zones help protect applications from data center failures and enable high availability and disaster recovery.

Azure   Active   Directory   (AAD)
A cloud-based identity and access management service from Microsoft. It provides features like single sign-on (SSO), multi-factor authentication (MFA), and access control for applications hosted on Azure and other services.

B

Bicep
A domain-specific language (DSL) for declarative Azure resource deployment. Bicep provides a simpler, more readable alternative to Azure Resource Manager (ARM) templates, allowing developers to define infrastructure as code.

Blob   Storage
A type of object storage in Azure used to store unstructured data, such as documents, images, videos, backups, and logs. Azure Blob Storage is highly scalable and durable.

Blue/Green   **Deployment**

A deployment strategy that reduces downtime and risk by running two identical production environments, called "blue" and "green." One environment is live (e.g., blue), while the other is idle or used for testing (e.g., green). The new version of the application is deployed to the green environment, and traffic is switched from blue to green once testing is successful.

C

Cloud   **Computing**

A model for delivering computing services (e.g., servers, storage, databases, networking, software) over the internet (the cloud), offering on-demand access to resources and services without the need for physical hardware.

CI/CD   **(Continuous**   **Integration/Continuous**   **Deployment)**

A set of practices that automate the process of integrating code changes, testing, and deploying them into production environments. CI/CD pipelines are essential for modern DevOps practices, allowing teams to deploy software quickly and reliably.

Containerization

A lightweight form of virtualization that involves encapsulating an application and its dependencies into a container. Containers can run consistently across different computing environments, enabling portability and scalability.

Cosmos   **DB**

A globally distributed, multi-model database service in Azure designed to provide low-latency, high-throughput data storage for mission-critical applications. It supports various data models, including document, graph, key-value, and column-family.

D

Data   **Lake**

A centralized repository that allows organizations to store structured, semi-structured, and unstructured data at any scale. Azure Data Lake is designed for big data analytics and can handle large volumes of diverse data types.

DevOps

A culture and set of practices that aim to shorten the software development lifecycle by fostering collaboration between development and operations teams. DevOps practices typically include automation, continuous integration, continuous delivery, and feedback loops.

Disaster   **Recovery**   **(DR)**

The process of recovering and restoring systems, applications, and data after a disaster, such as hardware failure, cyberattack, or natural disaster. Azure provides tools like **Azure Site Recovery** to help businesses implement disaster recovery strategies.

E

Event   **Grid**
An Azure service that enables event-driven architecture by providing a fully managed event routing service. Event Grid allows you to easily connect different services and trigger actions based on events, such as data updates, file uploads, or service failures.

Elastic   **Scaling**
The ability of a system or application to automatically scale resources up or down based on demand. In Azure, services like **Azure Virtual Machine Scale Sets** and **Azure App Service** support elastic scaling, ensuring resources are optimized to meet workload needs.

Elastic   **IP**
A static, public IPv4 address that can be dynamically reassigned to different Azure virtual machines. This is useful for high-availability applications that need a fixed IP address.

F

Function   **App**
An Azure service that allows you to run serverless applications. Azure Functions provide event-driven, compute-on-demand services, meaning that you only pay for the time your code is running.

Fault   **Tolerance**
The ability of a system or application to continue operating properly in the event of a hardware or software failure. Azure services like Availability Zones and region redundancy provide fault tolerance to ensure high availability.

G

GitHub   **Actions**
A feature of GitHub that enables continuous integration and continuous delivery (CI/CD) directly from GitHub repositories. It automates workflows, such as building, testing, and deploying applications, making it easier to implement DevOps practices.

Global   **Load**   **Balancer**
A service that distributes incoming network traffic across multiple resources, such as virtual machines, based on factors like geography or server health. Azure's **Traffic Manager** provides global load balancing capabilities to route traffic to the closest available resource.

H

High   **Availability**   **(HA)**
A design approach that ensures a system or application remains operational and accessible with minimal downtime, even in the event of hardware failures or outages. Azure provides various tools like Availability Sets and Availability Zones to implement HA solutions.

Hybrid   **Cloud**
A cloud architecture that combines on-premises infrastructure with public and/or private cloud services. Azure offers hybrid cloud solutions through services like **Azure Arc**, allowing organizations to manage and govern both on-premises and cloud resources seamlessly.

I

Infrastructure   **as**   **Code**   **(IaC)**
The practice of managing and provisioning computing infrastructure through machine-readable definition files, rather than physical hardware. Tools like **Terraform** and **Azure Resource Manager templates** allow you to define your infrastructure as code, automating the provisioning and management of cloud resources.

Identity   **and**   **Access**   **Management**   **(IAM)**
The framework and technologies used to manage user identities and control access to resources within an organization. In Azure, **Azure Active Directory (AAD)** is used to manage authentication and authorization for cloud-based applications.

J

JIT   **(Just-In-Time)**   **Access**
A security practice that provides temporary access to resources when needed, rather than granting persistent access. Azure **Privileged Identity Management (PIM)** allows for JIT access to Azure resources, enhancing security by minimizing exposure to sensitive data.

K

Kubernetes
An open-source platform for automating the deployment, scaling, and management of containerized applications. **Azure Kubernetes Service (AKS)** simplifies the deployment and management of Kubernetes clusters on Azure, providing scalability, security, and monitoring.

L

Load   **Balancer**
A network device or service that distributes incoming traffic across multiple servers or

instances to ensure no single server becomes overwhelmed. Azure provides **Azure Load Balancer** and **Azure Application Gateway** for distributing traffic within Azure resources.

Logic   Apps
 A fully managed service that allows you to automate workflows and integrate apps, data, and services. Logic Apps enable you to design workflows with a visual designer and integrate services such as Azure Functions, Office 365, and SQL databases.

M

Machine   Learning   (ML)
 A subset of artificial intelligence (AI) that involves training algorithms to learn from data and make predictions or decisions. **Azure Machine Learning** is a cloud service that helps data scientists build, train, and deploy machine learning models at scale.

Managed   Identity
 A feature in Azure that provides an automatically managed identity for applications to access Azure resources. Managed identities eliminate the need to store credentials in your code or configuration.

N

Network   Security   Group   (NSG)
 A network security feature that controls inbound and outbound traffic to Azure resources. NSGs allow you to define rules based on IP address, port, and protocol, ensuring only authorized traffic is allowed to reach your resources.

NAT   Gateway
 A service that enables secure and scalable outbound internet connectivity for resources in a Virtual Network. Azure **NAT Gateway** ensures that virtual machines and other resources have internet access without needing public IP addresses.

O

OAuth
 An open standard for access delegation that allows users to grant third-party applications access to their resources without sharing their credentials. Azure Active Directory (AAD) supports OAuth for user authentication and authorization.

Operational   Insights
 The process of gathering and analyzing data from an application's operations to improve performance, identify issues, and enhance overall system health. Azure **Monitor** provides

operational insights through data collected from application performance and resource metrics.

P

PowerShell
A task automation framework that provides a command-line interface for managing Azure resources. **Azure PowerShell** allows administrators to automate tasks such as resource provisioning, configuration, and monitoring.

Private   Link
A service in Azure that enables private, secure connections between Azure resources and services over a private network, eliminating the need for data to traverse the public internet.

Q

Query   Language
A language used to query databases or services for specific information. Azure **Kusto Query Language (KQL)** is used in Azure Monitor, Log Analytics, and Application Insights for querying and analyzing data.

R

Resource   Group
A container for managing and organizing related Azure resources. Resource groups allow you to manage resources collectively, apply security policies, and monitor usage.

Role-Based   Access   Control   (RBAC)
A method for managing access to resources in Azure. RBAC enables you to assign specific permissions to users or groups based on their roles within the organization.

S

Scaling
The process of adjusting the number of resources available to a system based on demand. **Vertical scaling** involves adding more resources to a single instance, while **horizontal scaling** involves adding more instances to distribute the load.

Serverless
A cloud computing model in which cloud providers automatically manage infrastructure,

allowing developers to focus on code without worrying about provisioning or managing servers. **Azure Functions** is an example of a serverless platform.

T

Terraform
An open-source IaC tool that allows you to define, provision, and manage cloud infrastructure using configuration files. **Terraform** integrates with Azure to automate the provisioning of resources in a declarative and repeatable way.

This glossary serves as a quick reference for understanding the key terms and concepts related to cloud computing, Azure, and DevOps practices. Familiarity with these terms will help you better navigate the world of cloud architecture and make more informed decisions as you design and deploy solutions on Azure.

Resources for Further Learning

In this section, we have compiled a comprehensive list of resources to help you deepen your understanding of Azure, cloud architecture, and DevOps practices. These resources include official documentation, courses, books, and community platforms that provide a wealth of knowledge to further enhance your skills.

1. Microsoft Learn

Microsoft Learn is a free, interactive platform that offers a wide range of learning paths and modules on Azure services, cloud computing, and DevOps. It's an excellent starting point for both beginners and experienced professionals. The platform provides hands-on labs, quizzes, and step-by-step guidance to help you gain practical experience.

- **Azure Fundamentals**: A beginner-level learning path that covers the core concepts of cloud computing and how Azure works.

- **Azure Developer**: Learn how to build and deploy applications on Azure using various Azure services like App Services, Functions, and Databases.

- **DevOps on Azure**: Learn how to implement CI/CD pipelines using Azure DevOps, Azure Pipelines, and other Azure DevOps services.

Visit: https://learn.microsoft.com/en-us/training/

2. Microsoft Azure Documentation

The official **Microsoft Azure Documentation** provides detailed, up-to-date guides and tutorials for all Azure services. Whether you are looking to understand how to set up a specific service or dive into advanced configurations, the Azure documentation is the authoritative source for all technical details and best practices.

- **Azure Overview**: The starting point for learning about all Azure services and their capabilities.

- **Azure Architecture Center**: A collection of architecture best practices, reference architectures, and design principles for building scalable and secure cloud solutions on Azure.

- **Azure SDKs and Tools**: Documentation on how to use SDKs and tools to interact with Azure resources using languages like Python, .NET, and JavaScript.

Visit: https://docs.microsoft.com/en-us/azure/

3. Azure DevOps Documentation

Azure DevOps provides a suite of tools for version control, build automation, release management, and project tracking. If you want to master DevOps practices on Azure, the Azure DevOps documentation is essential. It covers everything from getting started with Azure Repos, to configuring pipelines, to managing infrastructure with Infrastructure as Code (IaC).

- **Azure DevOps Introduction**: Learn the basics of Azure DevOps and how it integrates with Azure to enable a comprehensive DevOps pipeline.

- **CI/CD with Azure Pipelines**: A guide to setting up continuous integration and continuous delivery pipelines using Azure DevOps.

- **Managing Projects**: Understand how to manage agile projects using Azure Boards, track work items, and use backlog management.

Visit: https://docs.microsoft.com/en-us/azure/devops/

4. Books

1. *"Azure For Architects"* by Ritesh Modi

This book provides an in-depth exploration of Azure architecture, helping architects and developers design highly available, scalable, and secure cloud solutions. It covers the full

Azure ecosystem and provides insights into designing infrastructure for different types of workloads.

- Key topics include:
  - Design patterns for scalability and high availability.
  - Security considerations for cloud architectures.
  - Cost optimization strategies on Azure.

2. *"Designing Data-Intensive Applications"* by Martin Kleppmann

Although not Azure-specific, this book dives into building scalable and reliable data systems, an essential skill when working with cloud technologies like Azure. It provides the theoretical and practical knowledge needed to handle data at scale, covering topics like distributed systems, database consistency, and event-driven architecture.

- Key topics include:
  - Data models and databases (SQL vs. NoSQL).
  - Building scalable and reliable architectures.
  - Event-driven and microservices architectures.

3. *"Learning Azure DevOps"* by Michael J. K. Wright

For those looking to master DevOps practices with Azure, this book provides a comprehensive guide to Azure DevOps tools and services. It covers everything from managing source control with Git to implementing continuous integration and continuous delivery pipelines.

- Key topics include:
  - Setting up build and release pipelines.
  - Integrating with Azure Repos and GitHub.
  - Automating deployments to Azure services.

---

5. Online Learning Platforms

1. Pluralsight

Pluralsight offers high-quality courses on cloud computing, Azure, DevOps, and many other technology topics. It's an excellent platform for professionals who want structured learning paths and expert-led tutorials.

- **Azure Fundamentals**: A comprehensive series of courses for beginners that covers cloud computing basics and Azure services.

- **Azure DevOps**: A collection of courses dedicated to DevOps practices on Azure, including CI/CD, automation, and version control.

- **Advanced Azure Architectures**: Courses aimed at professionals who want to delve deeper into Azure's architectural best practices.

Visit: https://www.pluralsight.com/

2. Udemy

Udemy offers a wide variety of courses on Azure, DevOps, cloud computing, and software development. Courses are typically taught by industry professionals and include practical exercises and real-world examples.

- **Microsoft Certified: Azure Fundamentals Exam**: A course specifically designed to help you prepare for the Azure Fundamentals certification exam.

- **Azure DevOps Certification**: A course designed to help you understand how to use Azure DevOps to implement DevOps practices, from version control to deployment.

- **Advanced Azure Architectures**: A course for advanced users looking to design complex Azure infrastructures.

Visit: https://www.udemy.com/

3. LinkedIn Learning

LinkedIn Learning provides numerous courses on Azure and DevOps, catering to both beginner and advanced learners. The platform offers hands-on labs, video tutorials, and assessments to help learners grasp core concepts.

- **Azure Cloud Architect**: A series of courses designed to help you become proficient in designing cloud architectures on Azure.

- **DevOps with Azure**: Learn how to integrate Azure DevOps tools into your software development lifecycle.

- **Azure for Developers**: A course for developers looking to integrate Azure into their development practices, including using Azure Functions and App Services.

Visit: https://www.linkedin.com/learning/

---

6. Azure Community and Forums

1. Stack Overflow

Stack Overflow is an invaluable resource for developers working with Azure. It's a Q&A platform where you can find solutions to common issues and ask questions about any Azure-related challenges you're facing.

Visit: https://stackoverflow.com/questions/tagged/azure

2. Azure Community Forums

The **Azure Community Forums** are a great place to interact with other Azure professionals, share experiences, and get advice from experts. Whether you need help with specific Azure services or general cloud architecture design, the Azure forums are a helpful resource.

Visit: https://techcommunity.microsoft.com/t5/azure/

3. GitHub

GitHub is home to a vast number of open-source projects, including repositories for Azure architecture templates, DevOps scripts, and example code. Many Azure-related projects, including tools and SDKs, are hosted on GitHub, and you can collaborate with other developers to improve them.

Visit: https://github.com/Azure

---

7. Certifications

For those who want to validate their Azure expertise, Microsoft offers several certifications that demonstrate proficiency in various Azure and cloud technologies. These certifications can help you build credibility and advance your career in cloud computing and DevOps.

- **Microsoft Certified: Azure Fundamentals**: This certification is perfect for beginners who want to validate their foundational knowledge of cloud services and Azure.

- **Microsoft Certified: Azure Solutions Architect Expert**: This certification is aimed at professionals who want to demonstrate their ability to design and implement Azure architectures.

- **Microsoft Certified: Azure DevOps Engineer Expert**: A certification designed for professionals who want to validate their skills in DevOps practices, including continuous integration, delivery, and monitoring using Azure tools.

Visit: https://learn.microsoft.com/en-us/certifications/

Conclusion

The resources listed in this section offer a wealth of opportunities for anyone looking to deepen their knowledge of Azure, cloud architecture, and DevOps practices. Whether you are just starting with Azure or looking to enhance your expertise, these resources provide structured learning paths, real-world examples, and community support to help you grow as a cloud architect or DevOps engineer.

By leveraging these resources, you can stay up-to-date with the latest advancements in Azure and continue to build your skills in designing scalable, reliable, and secure cloud solutions.

Sample Projects and Code Snippets

In this section, we present a series of sample projects and code snippets that will help you apply the concepts covered throughout the book. These projects and code samples demonstrate practical use cases for building cloud applications, integrating Azure services, implementing DevOps practices, and working with various architectural patterns. These examples are intended to provide hands-on experience and serve as templates for your own projects.

1. Sample Project: Building a Serverless Web Application with Azure Functions

Overview:
 In this project, we will build a simple serverless web application using **Azure Functions**. The application will expose an HTTP endpoint that accepts input from users and stores the data in an Azure **Cosmos DB**. We will also deploy the application using **Azure DevOps**.

Steps:

1. **Create a New Azure Function App**:
   - First, create a new Azure Function App in the Azure portal.

```
az functionapp create --resource-group MyResourceGroup --consumption-plan-location eastus --runtime dotnet --name MyFunctionApp --storage-account mystorageaccount
```

2.

Write the Function: The function will be triggered by an HTTP request. It will accept JSON data and save it to Cosmos DB.

```csharp
 public static class HttpTriggerFunction
{
  [FunctionName("HttpTriggerFunction")]
  public static async Task<IActionResult> Run(
    [HttpTrigger(AuthorizationLevel.Function, "get", "post")] HttpRequestMessage req,
    [CosmosDB(
      databaseName: "UserData",
      collectionName: "Users",
      ConnectionStringSetting    =    "CosmosDBConnection")]    IAsyncCollector<User>
userCollection,
    ILogger log)
  {
    log.LogInformation("C# HTTP trigger function processed a request.");

    var user = await req.Content.ReadAsAsync<User>();
    await userCollection.AddAsync(user);

    return new OkObjectResult($"User {user.Name} added successfully.");
  }
}

public class User
{
  public string Id { get; set; }
  public string Name { get; set; }
  public int Age { get; set; }
}
```

3.
4. **Configure Cosmos DB**:
   Ensure that Cosmos DB is set up and that the connection string is added to the application settings in the Azure portal.

5. **Deploy Using Azure DevOps**:
   Set up an Azure DevOps pipeline for building and deploying the application.

   - **Create a Build Pipeline** in Azure DevOps that triggers on code commits.

   - **Create a Release Pipeline** that deploys the app to Azure after a successful build.

6. **Test the Application**:
   After deployment, test the application by sending a POST request to the Function URL with a JSON body containing user data.

2. Sample Project: Implementing Continuous Deployment with Azure DevOps

Overview:
This project demonstrates how to implement **continuous deployment (CD)** using **Azure DevOps** for a web application hosted in **Azure App Services**. We will create a pipeline that automatically deploys the latest version of the application after each commit.

Steps:

Set Up the Project: Create a simple **Node.js** web application using Express.

```
mkdir myapp
cd myapp
npm init -y
npm install express
```

Create a server.js file:

```
const express = require('express');
const app = express();
const port = process.env.PORT || 3000;

app.get('/', (req, res) => {
  res.send('Hello, Azure DevOps!');
});

app.listen(port, () => {
  console.log(`Server running at http://localhost:${port}`);
});
```

1.

Push to GitHub: Initialize a Git repository and push the application to GitHub.

```
git init
git add .
git commit -m "Initial commit"
git remote add origin https://github.com/yourusername/myapp.git
git push -u origin master
```

2.

Set Up Azure App Service: Create an Azure App Service to host the Node.js application.

```
az webapp create --resource-group MyResourceGroup --plan MyAppServicePlan --name MyNodeApp --runtime "NODE|12-lts"
```

3.

Set Up the Azure DevOps Pipeline: In Azure DevOps, create a new project and connect it to your GitHub repository. Then create a pipeline using the following YAML configuration:

```yaml
trigger:
  branches:
    include:
      - main

pool:
  vmImage: 'ubuntu-latest'

steps:
  - task: NodeTool@0
    inputs:
      versionSpec: '12.x'
      addToPath: true

  - script: |
      npm install
      npm run build
    displayName: 'Install dependencies and build'

  - task: AzureWebApp@1
    inputs:
      azureSubscription: 'MyAzureSubscription'
      appName: 'MyNodeApp'
      package: '$(System.DefaultWorkingDirectory)/myapp.zip'
```

4.
5. **Deploy Automatically**: Now, every time code is pushed to the main branch, Azure DevOps will automatically trigger the pipeline and deploy the updated code to Azure App   Service.

---

3. Sample Code Snippet: Auto-Scaling Virtual Machines in Azure

Overview:
 In this example, we will set up **auto-scaling** for **Azure Virtual Machines (VMs)** using the Azure CLI and ARM templates. Auto-scaling ensures that the number of VM instances adjusts dynamically based on demand.

Steps:

Create   a   Virtual   Machine   Scale   Set:

A **Virtual Machine Scale Set (VMSS)** enables you to manage a group of identical, load-balanced VMs. You can configure auto-scaling rules to add or remove instances based on resource utilization.

```
az vmss create \
 --resource-group MyResourceGroup \
 --name myScaleSet \
 --image UbuntuLTS \
 --upgrade-policy-mode automatic \
 --admin-username azureuser \
 --admin-password "Password123!" \
 --instance-count 2
```

1.

Configure Auto-Scaling: Set up auto-scaling to automatically adjust the number of instances based on CPU usage.

```
az vmss autoscale add \
 --resource-group MyResourceGroup \
 --name myScaleSet \
 --cpu-threshold 70 \
 --scale-in-threshold 30 \
 --scale-in-interval 10 \
 --scale-out-threshold 80 \
 --scale-out-interval 10 \
 --min-instances 1 \
 --max-instances 10
```

2.
3. **Test Auto-Scaling**: Simulate high CPU usage to trigger scaling out and low usage to trigger scaling in.

   o **Scale out**: When CPU usage exceeds 80%, Azure will automatically scale out the VMSS to a higher number of instances.

   o **Scale in**: When CPU usage falls below 30%, Azure will scale in the VMSS, reducing the number of instances.

---

4. Sample Project: Deploying a Microservices Architecture on Azure Kubernetes Service (AKS)

Overview:

This project demonstrates how to deploy a **microservices architecture** on **Azure Kubernetes Service (AKS)**. The microservices will be built using **Docker** and deployed to Kubernetes clusters using **Helm**.

Steps:

Set Up AKS Cluster:

Create an AKS cluster in the Azure portal or via the Azure CLI.

```
az aks create --resource-group MyResourceGroup --name myAKSCluster --node-count 3 --enable-addons monitoring --generate-ssh-keys
```

1.

Create Dockerized Microservices: Develop a set of microservices (e.g., a user service, an order service, and a payment service). Dockerize these services by creating Dockerfile files for each one.

Example Dockerfile for a Node.js application:

```
FROM node:14
WORKDIR /app
COPY . /app
RUN npm install
EXPOSE 3000
CMD ["npm", "start"]
```

2.

Build and Push Docker Images: Build Docker images for each microservice and push them to **Azure Container Registry (ACR)**.

```
docker build -t myacr.azurecr.io/userservice:latest .
docker push myacr.azurecr.io/userservice:latest
```

3.

Deploy with Helm: Use **Helm** to deploy the microservices on AKS. Create a Chart.yaml for the Helm chart and define Kubernetes deployment files for each service.

```
helm install mychart ./mychart
```

4.

Scale Microservices: Configure horizontal scaling for each microservice using Kubernetes **Horizontal Pod Autoscalers (HPA)**.

```
kubectl autoscale deployment userservice --cpu-percent=50 --min=1 --max=10
```

5.

6. **Monitor and Manage**: Use **Azure Monitor** and **Azure Log Analytics** to monitor the health and performance of the AKS cluster and the deployed microservices.

Conclusion

These sample projects and code snippets are designed to provide you with practical, hands-on experience working with Azure and implementing cloud-native solutions. By following these examples, you will learn how to deploy serverless applications, implement continuous deployment, manage auto-scaling virtual machines, and deploy microservices on Azure Kubernetes Service. These projects can also serve as starting points for your own production-level applications, helping you to quickly leverage Azure services and best practices in cloud architecture and DevOps.

API Reference Guide

This section provides an API reference guide for developers working with various Azure services and cloud architectures. Understanding how to interact with the Azure APIs allows developers to automate resource management, integrate services, and enhance the capabilities of their applications. The guide includes common API operations, examples, and best practices for working with key Azure services like **Azure Resource Manager (ARM)**, **Azure Active Directory (AAD)**, **Azure Storage**, **Azure Compute**, and **Azure DevOps**.

1. Azure Resource Manager (ARM) APIs

Azure Resource Manager (ARM) is the deployment and management service for Azure resources. It provides a unified and consistent management layer to manage your resources.

a. Creating a Resource Group

To begin managing Azure resources, you first need to create a **resource group**. A resource group is a logical container that holds related Azure resources.

```
POST /subscriptions/{subscriptionId}/resourceGroups?api-version=2021-04-01
```

Request Body:

```json
{
  "location": "eastus",
  "tags": {
    "environment": "production"
  }
}
```

Response:

```
{
  "id": "/subscriptions/{subscriptionId}/resourceGroups/myResourceGroup",
  "location": "eastus",
  "properties": {
    "provisioningState": "Succeeded"
  }
}
```

b. Creating a Virtual Machine (VM)

To create a virtual machine in a specific resource group:

```
PUT
/subscriptions/{subscriptionId}/resourceGroups/{resourceGroupName}/providers/Microsoft.C
ompute/virtualMachines/{vmName}?api-version=2021-03-01
```

Request Body:

```
{
  "location": "eastus",
  "properties": {
    "hardwareProfile": {
      "vmSize": "Standard_B1ms"
    },
    "storageProfile": {
      "osDisk": {
        "createOption": "FromImage",
        "managedDisk": {
          "storageAccountType": "Standard_LRS"
        }
      }
    },
    "osProfile": {
      "computerName": "myVM",
      "adminUsername": "adminuser",
      "adminPassword": "P@ssw0rd"
    },
    "networkProfile": {
      "networkInterfaces": [
        {
          "id":
"/subscriptions/{subscriptionId}/resourceGroups/{resourceGroupName}/providers/Microsoft.N
etwork/networkInterfaces/{nicName}"
```

```
        }
      ]
     }
    }
}
```

Response:

```
{
 "id":
"/subscriptions/{subscriptionId}/resourceGroups/{resourceGroupName}/providers/Microsoft.C
ompute/virtualMachines/myVM",
 "location": "eastus",
 "properties": {
   "provisioningState": "Succeeded"
 }
}
```

2. Azure Active Directory (AAD) APIs

Azure Active Directory (AAD) is Microsoft's cloud-based identity and access management service. It enables developers to authenticate users and manage access to applications and resources.

a. Get User Information

To retrieve user details from Azure AD, use the following API endpoint:

GET /v1.0/users/{userId}

Response:

```
{
 "id": "12345678-9abc-def0-1234-56789abcdef0",
 "userPrincipalName": "user@domain.com",
 "displayName": "John Doe",
 "mail": "john.doe@domain.com",
 "jobTitle": "Software Engineer",
 "department": "Engineering"
}
```

b. Creating a New User

To create a new user in Azure AD:

POST /v1.0/users

Request Body:

```
{
  "accountEnabled": true,
  "displayName": "Jane Smith",
  "userPrincipalName": "jane.smith@domain.com",
  "mailNickname": "janesmith",
  "passwordProfile": {
    "forceChangePasswordNextSignIn": true,
    "password": "SecureP@ssw0rd"
  }
}
```

Response:

```
{
  "id": "23456789-0abc-def1-2345-67890abcdef1",
  "userPrincipalName": "jane.smith@domain.com",
  "displayName": "Jane Smith",
  "jobTitle": "Project Manager"
}
```

3. Azure Storage APIs

Azure Storage provides several services for managing data, including **Blob Storage**, **Queue Storage**, **Table Storage**, and **File Storage**. The following examples show how to interact with **Blob Storage**.

a. Upload a Blob

To upload a blob to a container in Azure Blob Storage:

```
PUT https://{accountName}.blob.core.windows.net/{containerName}/{blobName}?{sasToken}
```

Headers:

```
x-ms-blob-type: BlockBlob
Content-Type: application/octet-stream
```

Request Body:

The content of the file you want to upload (e.g., a text file, image, etc.).

b. List Blobs in a Container

To list all the blobs in a container:

GET https://{accountName}.blob.core.windows.net/{containerName}?comp=list&{sasToken}

Response:

```xml
<?xml version="1.0" encoding="utf-8"?>
<ListBlobsResult>
  <Blobs>
    <Blob>
      <Name>blob1.txt</Name>
      <Properties>
        <LastModified>2021-09-01T00:00:00.0000000Z</LastModified>
        <ETag>"0x8D8D8C76F6D32D8"</ETag>
        <Content-Length>1024</Content-Length>
        <Content-Type>text/plain</Content-Type>
      </Properties>
    </Blob>
    <Blob>
      <Name>image.png</Name>
      <Properties>
        <LastModified>2021-09-02T00:00:00.0000000Z</LastModified>
        <ETag>"0x8D8D8C76F6D32D9"</ETag>
        <Content-Length>2048</Content-Length>
        <Content-Type>image/png</Content-Type>
      </Properties>
    </Blob>
  </Blobs>
</ListBlobsResult>
```

4. Azure Compute APIs

Azure Compute APIs are used to manage virtual machines, virtual machine scale sets, and other compute resources.

a. Start a Virtual Machine

To start a virtual machine:

POST
/subscriptions/{subscriptionId}/resourceGroups/{resourceGroupName}/providers/Microsoft.C
ompute/virtualMachines/{vmName}/start?api-version=2021-03-01

Response:

```
{
  "status": "OK",
  "message": "Virtual machine 'myVM' has been successfully started."
}
```

b. Stop a Virtual Machine

To stop a virtual machine:

```
POST
/subscriptions/{subscriptionId}/resourceGroups/{resourceGroupName}/providers/Microsoft.C
ompute/virtualMachines/{vmName}/deallocate?api-version=2021-03-01
```

Response:

```
{
  "status": "OK",
  "message": "Virtual machine 'myVM' has been successfully stopped."
}
```

5. Azure DevOps REST APIs

Azure DevOps provides a set of REST APIs for managing your DevOps workflows, including managing build pipelines, release pipelines, and work items.

a. Get Work Items

To retrieve a work item from Azure DevOps:

```
GET  https://dev.azure.com/{organization}/{project}/_apis/wit/workitems/{id}?api-version=7.1-
preview.1
```

Response:

```
{
  "id": 1234,
  "rev": 1,
  "fields": {
    "System.Title": "Fix bug in application",
    "System.State": "In Progress",
    "System.AssignedTo": {
      "displayName": "John Doe"
    }
```

```
    }
}
```

b. Create a Work Item

To create a new work item:

POST   https://dev.azure.com/{organization}/{project}/_apis/wit/workitems/${type}?api-version=7.1-preview.1

Request Body:

```
[
  {
    "op": "add",
    "path": "/fields/System.Title",
    "value": "Implement new feature"
  },
  {
    "op": "add",
    "path": "/fields/System.Description",
    "value": "Description of the feature implementation."
  }
]
```

Response:

```
{
  "id": 12345,
  "fields": {
    "System.Title": "Implement new feature",
    "System.Description": "Description of the feature implementation."
  }
}
```

6. Best Practices for API Usage

- **Authentication**: Always use OAuth 2.0 or **Azure Managed Identity** for secure authentication when accessing Azure APIs. For public-facing applications, ensure that credentials and keys are securely stored and not hardcoded in the application code.

- **Rate Limiting**: Be aware of rate limits imposed by Azure APIs. Always design your application to handle API throttling gracefully by implementing retries with exponential backoff.

- **Error Handling**: Ensure that you handle errors properly, especially for transient failures. Use appropriate HTTP status codes and try to provide clear error messages in your responses.

- **API Versioning**: Use versioning when calling APIs (e.g., /api-version=2021-03-01) to ensure compatibility with newer API versions and avoid breaking changes.

- **Logging and Monitoring**: Enable logging and monitoring on your API requests to capture and analyze usage, performance, and potential security incidents.

Conclusion

This API reference guide serves as a quick reference for interacting with key Azure services. By understanding these API calls, developers can automate cloud resource management, integrate services, and enhance their applications with advanced features. The code examples and best practices provided in this section will help you get started with building powerful cloud applications using Azure.

Frequently Asked Questions

This section provides answers to common questions regarding cloud architecture, Azure services, DevOps practices, and general best practices for designing scalable and secure cloud solutions. The goal is to address common issues, clarify confusing concepts, and provide practical tips for developers, architects, and DevOps professionals working with Azure.

1. What is Azure and why should I use it?

Azure is Microsoft's cloud computing platform, offering a wide range of services that include computing power, storage, databases, machine learning, networking, and more. It enables organizations to build, deploy, and manage applications and services through Microsoft-managed data centers.

Reasons to use Azure:

- **Scalability**: Easily scale applications up or down to meet the demands of your business.

- **Global Reach**: With data centers across the globe, Azure allows for high availability and low latency.

- **Security**: Azure provides robust security features, including encryption, multi-factor authentication, and compliance with industry standards like HIPAA, GDPR, and more.

- **Integration**: Seamlessly integrates with existing Microsoft products like Office 365, Dynamics 365, and other enterprise software.

- **Cost Efficiency**: Azure offers pay-as-you-go pricing models, allowing businesses to reduce upfront capital expenses and optimize their IT costs.

---

2. What is Infrastructure as Code (IaC), and why is it important?

Infrastructure as Code (IaC) is a practice in which infrastructure is managed and provisioned using code and automation tools. IaC allows you to define your infrastructure through code rather than manual configuration, which makes it easier to version control, automate, and replicate environments.

Why is IaC important?:

- **Automation**: Automates the provisioning and configuration of resources, reducing manual intervention and the risk of human error.

- **Consistency**: Ensures that environments are consistent across all stages (development, testing, production) by using the same code to provision resources.

- **Scalability**: Easily replicate environments across regions or environments for scaling up or testing.

- **Versioning**: Track changes to infrastructure over time and roll back to previous configurations if necessary.

Example of IaC using Terraform for creating an Azure Virtual Machine:

```
provider "azurerm" {
  features {}
}

resource "azurerm_virtual_machine" "example" {
  name                 = "myVM"
  location             = "East US"
  resource_group_name  = azurerm_resource_group.example.name
  network_interface_ids = [azurerm_network_interface.example.id]
  vm_size              = "Standard_B1ms"

  os_profile {
    computer_name = "hostname"
```

```
  admin_username = "adminuser"
  admin_password = "P@ssw0rd"
}

os_profile_windows_config {
  provision_vm_agent = true
  enable_automatic_upgrades = true
}
}
```

---

3. What is the difference between Azure Compute Services: VMs, App Services, and Containers?

Azure provides various compute services to suit different application types. Here's a comparison of the three major types of compute services:

- **Virtual Machines (VMs)**: VMs are the most flexible form of compute resource in Azure. They provide an entire virtualized server, giving full control over the operating system, installed software, and network configurations. VMs are ideal for running legacy applications or applications that need to be fully customized.

  Use Case: Running custom applications or software that requires full control over the underlying operating system.

- **App Services**: Azure App Services is a platform-as-a-service (PaaS) offering that allows you to host web applications, APIs, and mobile backends. It abstracts away the underlying infrastructure, allowing developers to focus on coding and not on managing the operating system or hardware.

  Use Case: Hosting web applications, REST APIs, and mobile backends.

- **Containers (AKS)**: Containers allow you to package an application and its dependencies in a lightweight, portable format that can run consistently across any environment. Azure Kubernetes Service (AKS) is a managed service for running containers at scale, with support for orchestrating containerized applications.

  Use Case: Running microservices-based applications or applications that need to be highly portable and scalable.

---

4. What are the best practices for securing my Azure resources?

Security is critical when building cloud-based applications and systems. Azure offers a variety of security features and best practices to help protect your resources. Some of the best practices include:

1. **Use Azure Active Directory (AAD) for Identity and Access Management (IAM)**: Manage user identities and control access to resources using Azure AD.

2. **Enable Multi-Factor Authentication (MFA)**: Use MFA to add an extra layer of protection for user accounts, especially for administrators and users with access to sensitive   data.

3. **Use Role-Based Access Control (RBAC)**: Assign permissions based on the role of the user rather than granting blanket permissions. This ensures that users only have access   to   the   resources   they   need.

4. **Use Network Security Groups (NSGs)**: Restrict access to virtual machines and other Azure   resources   by   defining   inbound   and   outbound   traffic   rules.

5. **Encrypt Data**: Use Azure encryption features for data at rest and in transit. Azure provides encryption for both platform-managed and customer-managed keys.

6. **Regularly Review Access Logs**: Use **Azure Monitor** and **Azure Security Center** to monitor and audit access logs for suspicious activity and non-compliance.

---

5. What is the role of Azure DevOps in a modern cloud architecture?

Azure DevOps is a suite of development tools that helps teams automate and streamline the software development lifecycle. It includes tools for version control, build automation, release management, testing, and monitoring. Azure DevOps integrates well with Azure services, making it a powerful tool for managing cloud-native applications.

Key components of Azure DevOps:

- **Azure Repos**: A source control service that supports Git repositories for versioning code.

- **Azure Pipelines**: A CI/CD service for automating build, test, and deployment workflows.

- **Azure Boards**: A project management tool that supports Agile, Scrum, and Kanban workflows   for   tracking   tasks   and   issues.

- **Azure Artifacts**: A package management service to share and manage dependencies like   NuGet,   npm,   and   Maven   packages.

Benefits of using Azure DevOps:

- **Automation**: Automates repetitive tasks such as building, testing, and deploying applications.

- **Collaboration**: Promotes collaboration between development, operations, and QA teams.

- **Consistency**: Ensures consistent environments by using IaC and configuration management.

Example of setting up a CI/CD pipeline in Azure DevOps using YAML:

```
trigger:
  branches:
    include:
      - main

pool:
  vmImage: 'ubuntu-latest'

steps:
- task: NodeTool@0
  inputs:
    versionSpec: '14.x'
    addToPath: true

- script: |
    npm install
    npm run build
  displayName: 'Install dependencies and build'

- task: AzureWebApp@1
  inputs:
    azureSubscription: 'MyAzureSubscription'
    appName: 'MyWebApp'
    package: '$(System.DefaultWorkingDirectory)/myapp.zip'
```

6. How can I monitor the health and performance of my Azure resources?

Azure provides several monitoring tools and services to help you keep track of the health and performance of your resources. The key services include:

- **Azure Monitor**: A comprehensive service for monitoring the performance and health of your applications, VMs, and Azure resources. It provides a central location for collecting metrics, logs, and diagnostic data.

- **Application Insights**: Part of Azure Monitor, Application Insights is designed for monitoring live web applications. It provides telemetry on performance, exceptions, and usage patterns, helping you identify bottlenecks and errors in your application.

- **Azure Security Center**: A unified security management system that helps detect and respond to security threats across your Azure resources. It provides a dashboard for managing security policies, alerts, and recommendations.

- **Azure Log Analytics**: A tool for querying and analyzing log data across your Azure resources. It integrates with Azure Monitor and provides advanced analytics capabilities to help identify trends and anomalies.

7. What is the difference between Azure Blob Storage and Azure File Storage?

Both **Azure Blob Storage** and **Azure File Storage** provide cloud storage solutions, but they are designed for different use cases:

- **Azure Blob Storage** is designed for storing unstructured data, such as documents, images, videos, backups, and log files. It is optimized for high-throughput, low-latency access to large amounts of data.

  Use Cases:

  - Storing images, videos, or any type of unstructured data.

  - Backups and disaster recovery.

  - Big data analytics and log storage.

- **Azure File Storage** provides a fully managed **Network Attached Storage (NAS)** in the cloud. It is ideal for scenarios where you need to mount a shared file system to multiple virtual machines.

  Use Cases:

  - Storing configuration files or application data that needs to be accessed by multiple VMs.

  - Lift-and-shift scenarios where you need to move on-premises applications to the cloud that rely on shared file storage.

Conclusion

This FAQ section aims to answer some of the most common questions regarding Azure and cloud computing. From foundational concepts like the difference between Azure services to practical solutions for security, monitoring, and DevOps, these answers provide insights that can guide your journey in using Azure effectively. If you have additional questions, don't hesitate to explore the official Azure documentation or community forums for further clarification.